RELATIONSHIP MATTERS

RELATIONSHIP MATTERS

A New Paradigm for an Evolutionary Leap in Relationships

FAITH FULLER, PHD, ORSCC

Foreword by
Marita Fridjhon, MSW, ORSCC

PRAISE

"All things, from molecules to people, to galaxies, are bound together through relationship. This book suggests we can be more conscious and intentional about how we connect with each other and our world. By increasing our relational skills and awareness, Faith shows how to make crucial steps toward the needed personal and social changes."

Drs. Amy and Arnold Mindell, Founders of the Process Work Institute

"So much, if not all, of what we as humanity face boils down to how we relate to one another—whether that be in business, to one's partner, or to one's self, for that matter. Faith and Marita have a unique approach to unlocking the path forward in these domains rooted in their therapeutic as well as counseling backgrounds while also being informed by their deep and rich life experiences. This is a MUST read."

Stephen Badger, former Chairman and Current Board Member of Mars Incorporated

"What is remarkable about *Relationship Matters* is that it looks underneath the surface of relationship and provides a clear and engaging context for a deeper understanding that we can leverage to grow ourselves and our world, to inform and transform. In personal, provocative, profound, and pragmatic ways, this book provides much-needed vision and inspiration that will be priceless for anyone working in the human development field or who values human development personally."

Karen Kimsey-House, CPCC, Cofounder and Board Chair, the Co-Active Training Institute

"When I was introduced to the content of *Relationship Matters* in 2012, I held relationships at work as secondary to the job. As an ambitious government employee in a large county in the San Francisco Bay Area, I was a 'doer' who could sometimes push others to implement my vision. The problem was that this approach often proved unsuccessful because I was neglecting many voices in the system (even some of my own)! Faith taught me, as well as many others in my organization, that attending to all levels of relationship and the system within those relationships are primary and essential for effecting change.

The tools and concepts revealed in *Relationship Matters* not only allowed my department to heal from challenging times, but also helped us to increase joy and productivity in our work together."

Lisa Warhuus, PhD, ORSCC, Director of Health,
Housing, and Community Services, City of Berkeley

"So often, we hear the word *relationship,* and a married couple comes to mind. As a university professor and department chair, I know that healthy relationships are critical for student success in the classroom and faculty interactions with students and colleagues. I lean into the tenets of *Relationship Matters* by incorporating a multitude of exercises into my classroom and faculty interactions. It is nothing short of miraculous to see how new-found self-awareness and empathy enriches every student and faculty interaction. Without question, Faith's work has made me a better department chair—one capable of developing faculty and navigating the politics and thorniest issues in higher education.

*Vicki Purslow, EdD, MA, Music Dept. Chair and
Professor of Music at Southern Oregon University*

"Faith's book, *Relationships Matters*, is full of deep wisdom and practical insight. Faith has the unique ability to skillfully cut to the heart of an issue and offers valuable tools for both personal growth and growth in relationship. This book will benefit anyone interested in being challenged in the most important parts of our lives and relationships.

"Faith has coached us to improve our relationships with our colleagues, our children, and each other. If you're looking to deepen relationships and better understand yourself, lean into the useful and thought-provoking questions proposed at the end of each chapter. We are forever grateful to Faith for this book and for her life-changing work in our lives."

Andy Grove, MA, Assistant Chief, Kent Police Department

*Hanna Grove, Coaching Mastery Certificate CRM,
Coach for Beyond Brilliant, Provident Heights*

"Recently, I was involved with a project with a colleague who seemed to be dragging his feet with deliverables for our agreed-upon timeline. As I found myself getting more and more frustrated, I remembered what I learned about being in a 'system' and 'Emotional EQ' from *Relationship Matters*. As I applied these principles to my situation, I could see that our processes, styles, abilities, and needs were very different. As I realized this, my frustration levels dropped, my empathy raised, and I was able to approach my colleague in a constructive way about how we could work together more effectively. The outcome was that he was very open to the discussion, and our working relationship is better than ever. Thank you for this incredible book and the wisdom within its pages."

Howard VanEs, President, Let's Write Books, Inc.

"This book is deeply personal, global, and universal. Faith gently reminds us about our dreams and longings for relationships in our life, and passionately invites us to walk the path of Relationship Warriorship. The wisdom written in this book is 100 percent applicable to any leaders and professionals around the world. I could not imagine myself standing in complex issues and difficult emotional fields without the teaching of Relationship Systems Intelligence."

Yuri Morikawa, ORSCC, CPCC, MCC, Founder of CRR Global Japan

"Are you ready for a powerful and provocative invitation? Faith Fuller invites us to engage in the mystery, challenge, and responsibility of having our relationships work. Not only does she state the case for this evolution, but she literally shows us how to do the work. As an 'ORSC' practitioner myself, I was lucky to be among the first to learn and teach this work in the early 2000s. In fact, this work was the main inspiration for my Inside Team concept and the book that I wrote. Now, twenty years later, Faith's words reawaken me and call me forth to continued Relationship Warriorship. Thank you, Faith (and Marita)!"

Cynthia Loy Darst, CPCC, ORSCC, MCC
Author of Meet Your Inside Team: How to Turn Internal
Conflict into Clarity *and* Move Forward with Your Life

"I had so much fun reading this book! Equipped with paper and coloring pens, I discovered new aspects of who I am and, with a renewed curiosity, observed the business partnership that leads this training, coaching, and consultancy business. Most fascinating was stepping into the relationship voice and feeling, sensing, and becoming aware of something so profoundly different than my/our voice! With the help of this book, I will be inviting the team that leads the organisation in a conversation about how we can take co-responsibility to create a culture that serves and expands our diversity.

"First step . . . to have a conversation on Monday about our morning ritual!"

Nairy McMahon, CPCC, ORSCC, Director and
Founder of CRR Global UK

"Faith Fuller is an authority in the world of relationship. She is also my personal role model for how to walk the path of right relationship. This book offers a powerful combination of deep relationship wisdom as well as tools and exercises for how to bring that alive. By practicing ourselves, we learn best after all. The piece that spoke to me most was the concept of Radical Responsibility, of getting beyond blame and looking into the question, 'What is my part in what is happening.' If that's the only concept you take from this book, we will be able to work our egos and serve the world."

Judy van Zon, CPCC, ORSCC, CRR Global Faculty Since 2010,
Former Director of Certification CRR Global

"This is the best book I have read in a long time on how to intentionally be in and work with relationships. This is a must-read for leaders, therapists, coaches, and relational warriors on how to help evolve the world today."

Michael Holton, CPCC, ORSCC

"'We don't know who we are without relationship,' is such a profound statement coming from Faith Fuller's new book, *Relationship Matters*. We work the entirety of our lives navigating relationships whether we hold consciousness around this or not. Faith takes us into the experience of our lives, showing us how we are always intimately in relationships with ourselves first and then with others. Humans are complex multi-dimensional beings, and as Faith expresses, we are constantly negotiating these complexities within ourselves and within the relationship systems to which we belong . . . moment by moment. We need these levels of awareness of ourselves and our connection to others to meet the needs of the complexities of the power imbalances and systemic equities—race, ethnicity, religion, sexual orientation, gender, etc.—in our world today."

Michelle Davis, MS, ORSCC, LPC

Relationship Matters

A New Paradigm for an Evolutionary Leap in Relationships

Faith Fuller, PhD, ORSCC

Published by CRR Global
ISBN 978-1-7374976-2-2
Library of Congress Number 2023922793

Published in Benecia, CA

FOREWORD

I met Faith for the first time in 1991 in San Francisco when working as a consultant for Joanna Macy, a renowned spiritual teacher and nature advocate. Faith was living on the East Coast and helming an initiative with Joanna that brought together activists to work on creating action and awareness around climate change. This resulted in a group of activists coming together in Berkeley, CA, with the goal of scaling this important work. Faith was one of the main players working with Joanna and organizing this mission. We spent several days together with an amazing group of colleagues navigating the future of global climate change from a systemic perspective.

Why this story at the beginning of this remarkable book written by Faith? Because at the end of that gathering, something happened when I took Faith to the airport for her flight back to Baltimore. As I sat chatting with her at the gate before boarding, I was aware of something I had never experienced before . . . a vision of the future, still shrouded in the mystery of not knowing. I had a sense of intimacy, love, and purpose so strong I literally felt confused and a bit lost. Faith's boarding call brought me back to myself as she got up to walk through the gate. We hugged goodbye. Then out of the blue, she turned, took my face in her hands, kissed me, and said, "You know this is inevitable, right?" Then she turned around and walked through the door. Why this story here? Because that was the start of our journey together, co-creating the "inevitable" gift and legacy of relationship systems coaching. Relationships do, indeed, matter.

This book is the culmination of a journey of two women, from different global backgrounds, who came together after divorce and complicated relationship histories to share a thirty-two-year life and marriage. It is about what we learned from our teams, organizations, family, and couples' work as we built CRR Global. It also highlights the humble truth that family is the final exam of right relationship. It is "easy" to train and coach partnerships and teams. However, walking the talk with your own spouse, family, or team is frustrating, humbling, and, indeed, a spiritual journey. Even after thirty-two years, our refrigerator is covered with encouraging sticky notes and quotes from our own material. They are reminders like: "Find right first." "Listen with questions, not answers." "Meet people where they are—not where you think they should be!" They are a testament to marriage as the final exam.

This book is full of multiple perspectives and stories from science, spirituality, psychology, and more. They illustrate how CRR Global trains in Organization and Relationship Systems Coaching (ORSC). The global impact of this systems-inspired work has been remarkable in cultures ranging from Africa to Asia, Europe, the Middle East, and more. Our global faculty in eighteen different countries and at least five different languages have created a global ripple effect. It illustrates the reality that relationship matters—from the living room to the bedroom, to the street, to nature, and more. The data and examples listed in the book also highlight our experience and challenges from the perspective of being co-founders of a global training company and thought leaders in the coaching and consulting business. The book tracks much of our journey through a global recession, COVID, and more.

Relationships are **the** most valuable currency in the evolutionary journey for humanity and nature because it is the foundation for everything.

Through stories, examples, and thought questions, you will be invited to explore the deep complexity of your own human relationships.

This book invites you into being in relationship with it. How will you choose to read it? From beginning to end? Picking certain chapters that got your attention? This will depend on your style, where you find yourself in your own life challenges, whether you have done any of the training offered through CRR Global, and more. Trust and follow your own judgment and intuition. One thing that we do know is that there is no final goalpost in the journey to right relationship! Relationship intricacy and richness increase as our own vertical development deepens, and the challenges and opportunities we face bring ever more complexity. Being in relationship is an infinite game. Dive into the examples, skills, and tools here and find ways to apply them to tired grocery store clerks, to your toddler, or to teams when they are melting down. Get curious about the unique personality (or Third Entity) holding your marriage. Think about a conflict in your life and hunt for the tools to help create alignment.

One of the biggest challenges in our society today is the emerging boundaryless nature of change. We not only experience an unprecedented increase in the speed of change, but change itself is evolving. We only need to look at nature and global climate change, the emergence of AI, global cultural shifts, and more to become aware of the increased complexity of what change means. Despite all of that, one thing remains central to the ability and evolution of *how* to navigate this boundaryless emergence of change, and that is being in relationship with, and to, all of it. Dare to be brave and say yes to relationship as the key to opening new possibilities and commit to the reality that relationship matters!

Welcome to the journey.

Marita Fridjhon, MSW, ORSCC

For you, reader, who carry the torch forward.

CONTENTS

Symbols   xv

INTRODUCTION   1

CHAPTER 1   What Made You Pick Up This Book?   3

CHAPTER 2   Who Are We to Write This Book?   7

CHAPTER 3   Developmental History of Relationship Systems
             Coaching   9

CHAPTER 4   How to Read This Book   14

PART 1   THE BASICS   17

CHAPTER 5   The Model   19

CHAPTER 6   Everything Is Relationship   29

CHAPTER 7   Relationship Systems   33

CHAPTER 8   Levels of Relationship   36

CHAPTER 9   The Third Entity   44

CHAPTER 10   How Are You Intelligent?   66

PART 2   **THE PRINCIPLES OF RSI**   **105**

CHAPTER 11   Introduction to the Principles – How Relationship
             Systems Behave   107

CHAPTER 12   Principle – Every Relationship System Is Unique   110

CHAPTER 13   Principle – Systems Are in a Constant State of
             Emergence   123

CHAPTER 14   Principle – Every Member of a Relationship System
             Is a Voice of the System (Vos)   143

CHAPTER 15   Principle – Systems Are Naturally Intelligent,
             Creative, and Generative   155

CHAPTER 16   Principle – Systems Rely on Roles for Their
             Organization and Execution of Functions   181

PART 3   **EVOLUTION THROUGH RELATIONSHIP**   **215**

             Epilogue   217

About CRR Global   227
About the Author   229
Acknowledgments   230
Bibliography   232

SYMBOLS

Symbol	Description
	Definitions and Ideas
	Story
	Exercises

INTRODUCTION

CHAPTER 1

WHAT MADE YOU PICK UP THIS BOOK?

We're curious. What made you pick up this book? Certainly, you have relationships in your life. You probably have a family, co-workers, and are part of your local community. Maybe you deal with relationships professionally, as a coach or consultant? Maybe you are a lifelong learner, and you want to grow. But there's something that made you think that this book might be relevant for you.

This book is about evolution through relationship. It is about how the relationships in our lives—at work, at home, and in our country—are a major force for personal and societal transformation. The good news is that we live in a sea of relationships, and all those connections are constantly making us grow.

As humans, we are at a critical inflection point in our development. Over the past fifty years, we've seen extraordinary advancements in technology and science, with information doubling every eighteen to twenty-four months (Bell, 2016). Yet now, the 1965 theory, known as Moore's Law, which has correctly predicted exponential processor transistor growth (or, put simply, the amount of computer power we can squeeze into even smaller devices), is starting to slow down. In a 2018 article for *Medium*, Steve Blank suggests that we are "at the end of the beginning" in terms of technical growth. We've reached an end in terms of the **type** of technological innovation we have been developing and using for the last sixty years. So, beyond Moore's law, what might the next era of human innovation and evolution look like? We believe the next area of human development needs to be **relational.**

We are extraordinary technology problem solvers, but we are not so good at getting along with each other. Here are some examples:

- The likelihood of your marriage ending in divorce is about 39 percent (Felsenthal, 2020).

- Employees in US companies spend approximately 2.8 hours each week involved in conflict. This amounts to around $359 billion in hours paid that are filled with and focused on conflict instead of positive, productive work (U.S. Bureau of Labor Statistics).

- One in three women globally experience domestic violence (World Health Organization).

- Half a million people each year are killed by interpersonal violence. That's 1,300 people each day, or nine times the number of lives lost in open warfare (United Nations)!

- At least 108 million people were killed in wars in the twentieth century, and there are more than forty active conflicts going on in the world at the time of writing.

This data is depressing, but it isn't surprising. Our understanding of interactions between people is incredibly primitive. Psychology, which is the study of the mind and behavior, is only about 120 years old.[1] Social

---

1 Freudian psychology was founded in 1900.

Psychology and couples work is even younger. It wasn't until the early 1950s that therapists began working with psychological issues in the family (Nichols & Davis, 2019). From first grade, we are trained in writing, computers, science, and history. But generally, there are no courses called Relationships 101, Advanced Training in Having Constructive Conflict, or Learning from the Opposing Political Party.

So, as a species, we are armed to the teeth with devasting weapons, while also having very little training in how to get along with other people. It's not a great combination.

HANDCUFFS & KNIVES

Sometimes, relationships feel like being handcuffed together with someone who is holding a knife in the other hand. As the adage goes: "Loving someone is giving them the power to destroy you but trusting them not to." This is why we believe that our very road to survival as a species now needs to develop along the lines of better relationship skills.

So, how do we become better spouses, parents, bosses, and citizens? How do we evolve our understanding of ourselves, the people we care about, and collective systems like teams, organizations, and countries?

This book has an invitation; **join us in supporting the world through evolving better relationships.** If you are sometimes brokenhearted and frustrated by how humans relate to each other and the planet, this book is for you. Does it mean this book has all the relationship answers? Of course not! No book or even a library of books has all the answers. Relationships remain a great mystery.

However, we do have a model for how to evolve human relationships. The next step to getting started is something called Relationship Warriorship. A Relationship Warrior is someone who believes relationships matter and has the tools and skills to achieve the goal of what we call Right Relationship. Below is a brief model for this book, which we will further flesh out in the Basics Chapter.

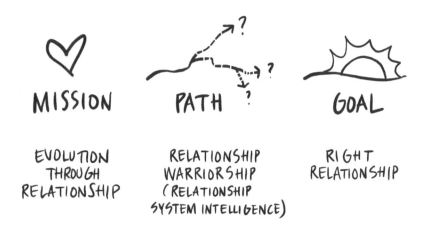

MISSION   PATH ?   GOAL

EVOLUTION THROUGH RELATIONSHIP   RELATIONSHIP WARRIORSHIP (RELATIONSHIP SYSTEM INTELLIGENCE)   RIGHT RELATIONSHIP

The only prerequisite to reading this book is that you be in relationships, and that is pretty much everyone. If your life is touched by the relationships in your life, by the struggles with your teams, the joy in your kids, and your hope for a better future together, then this book can help you upskill your relationships.

CHAPTER 2

WHO ARE WE TO WRITE THIS BOOK?

My name is Faith Fuller, and I am the primary voice of this book. I am speaking on behalf of a host of others, including my spouse Marita Fridjhon, and the thousands of students who have shaped this work. I am a PhD. Psychologist, a coach, and a consultant. Marita and I are the founders of CRR Global, an ICF-accredited ACTP coach training school, and creators of the Organizational and Relationship Systems Coaching Program (ORSC).

For over eighteen years, CRR Global has accompanied leaders, teams, and practitioners on their journey to build stronger relationships. This led to a community of changemakers around the world. This book leverages the wisdom of a global network of faculty, partners, families, and organizations. Without those relationships, this book would not exist. At CRR Global, we believe that **relationship matters, from the board room to the bedroom.**[2]

---

2   Some readers may remember the old CRR Global tagline: 'From the boardroom to the living room we believe Relationship Matters." We originally wanted it to read "from the board room to the bedroom" to include intimate relationships, but in the end, we changed it, so not to scare away the organizations we were working with! That said, we hope you enjoy this reference, which spans from professional to the very personal.

To write this book, we stand on the shoulders of giants. We would like to respectfully honor the many contributors to this work, including psychology, coaching, organizational development, process work, and conflict resolution.[3] Our work draws from many sources, and one of our abilities is the capacity to integrate many perspectives into a more cohesive whole. You will find the threads of many disciplines in this book, and we are proud to be part of the tapestry of relationship wisdom contributors.

We also want to acknowledge that our work is written from a particular perspective. Marita and I are white women, and we are aware that our voices cannot help but reflect the biases, blind spots, and privileges of our relatively affluent culture. We are also older, and two women married to each other. Relationship cannot be understood separately from its context. Notice where this book fits and where it does not, with your own culture and experience. This book is a collaboration with you. We will open the conversation about relationship from our understanding. We are leaning into **you** to further the work from your own personal and societal experience. We hope you will stand on our shoulders to adapt this work to your cultural perspectives just as we have stood on the shoulders of others. A universal experience for all of us is that relationships get under our skin and force us to grow.

---

3   Process-oriented psychology was developed by Arnold Mindell, a physicist and Jungian analyst, and has its roots in Jungian psychology, physics, and Taoism. The Taoist view of life assumes that the way things unfold contains the basic elements necessary for solving human problems. Process Work, like Taoism, is about the "unfolding" of what is happening. Process work holds that relationships are living entities and act as teachers for individual transformation.

CHAPTER 3

DEVELOPMENTAL HISTORY OF RELATIONSHIP SYSTEMS COACHING

"Life is better when we are connected."

– BANK OF AMERICA

As the above slogan indicates, relationships are trending. We have always known the impact of family relationships in our lives. Now, the importance of "social capitol," such as relationships at work, is being backed up by research.[4]

---

4   In 2012, Google embarked on an initiative—code-named Project Aristotle—to uncover what makes the perfect team. They looked at over 180 teams and had lots of data, but there was nothing showing that a mix of specific personality types or skills or backgrounds made any difference. The "who" part of the equation didn't seem to matter. It seems there is no magic ingredient for perfecting relationships!

In a 2019 article for Harvard Business Review, Rob Cross writes: "Studies show that social connections play a central role in fostering a sense of purpose and well-being in the workplace." Cross found that flourishing in your career depends as much on your relationships as it does on the job itself. The article goes on to say that social capital "facilitates learning and knowledge sharing, increases employee retention and engagement, reduces burnout, sparks innovation, and improves employee and organizational performance."[5]

This focus on relationship hasn't always been the case. When Marita and I founded CRR Global, relationships were far from trending, at least not professionally. Back in the nineties, when we started this work, organizations were all about productivity. Leanness. How do you squeeze more out of less—whether it's people, tasks, or materials? CEOs were actually confused when we talked to them about Relationship Systems. After all, what did relationships have to do with productivity? From their work perspective, relationships were messy, unprofessional, and something to be avoided if possible. Relationships brought up emotion and emotion should be left at the office door.

COACHING, THERAPY, OR SOMETHING ELSE?

The coaching industry's focus during this time was on individual or executive coaching. The CRR in our company name stands for the Center for Right Relationship. This name was so alarming to businesses that we changed it to CRR Global. Everybody knew that relationships were a part of life coaching because they were an important part of life. But few coaches

---

5   After interviewing 160 people from a variety of industries and positions, the Harvard Business Review study found that "flourishing in your career depends as much on your relationships, both in and out of work, as it does on your job itself" (Cross, 2019).

had any training at all on working with relationships. Relationships were left to the therapists at the time. When our coaching school was accredited by The International Coaching Federation (ICF), they required that we write a whitepaper on the difference between Coaching and Therapy. Marita and I had our roots in the mental health industry, so this was easy for us. There are, of course, both overlap and major differences between doing therapy and relationship systems coaching.[6]

Therapy and Counselling:	*Relationship Systems Coaching:*
Focus on mental health issues	Focus on human development
Problem-orientated	Goal-orientated
Work with the past and present	Works with the present and paves the way for the future
Primarily work with individuals and families	Works with individuals, families, and organizational systems

Both these modalities can respect and support their different perspectives and often cross-refer to one another.

THE BLEEDING EDGE

So, back in the nineties, we weren't on the cutting edge of coaching or relationship work. We were on what we call the "bleeding edge." In other words, we were a stretch for people because it was difficult for them to understand why relationship might matter, particularly in the workplace.

Much of that changed when the leadership movement came in. CEOs and HR Managers initially didn't understand the connection between

---

6   You can read the Whitepaper here: https://crrglobal.com/wp-content/uploads/attachments/creating_coaching_cultures_guide.2016_4.pdf.

BLEEDING EDGE

personal interactions and productivity, but once the leadership movement arrived, everyone understood that good leadership requires
good relationship skills. You cannot influence, inspire, and lead people
without having good relationship skills.

Marita and I knew that relationship mattered, even when we were on the
bleeding edge. Nevertheless, we persisted! Today, relationship issues are
a major theme in individual coaching, and team coaching is one of the
fastest-growing areas of the coaching profession. In fact, by the end of
2020, the International Coaching Federation released its Team Coaching
Competencies Model, defining team coaching as "an experience that
allows a team to work towards sustainable results and ongoing development. It is becoming an increasingly important intervention in corporate
environments as high team performance requires aligning toward goals,
remaining innovative, and adapting quickly to internal and external

changes."[7] One estimate suggests that the world will need over 150,000 new team coaches over the next five years.

The coaching and consulting professions now recognize the importance of relationships. However, CRR Global is probably still on the bleeding edge in terms of our commitment. We believe relationships are a **primary** channel for personal and societal evolution.

We are just beginning to learn what is beneath the surface of relationships. When the first crude microscope was developed hundreds of years ago, the curious were astonished by the wealth of "animalcules" within a drop of pond water. There was a whole world of creatures, plants, and structures that had always been there but couldn't be seen. Similarly, we are just learning about the complexity of relationships. We are all relative beginners at relationships; we haven't had much training. This book is about making invisible relationship issues visible.

---

7   A critical distinction between the ICF Core Competencies and the ICF Team Coaching Competencies is the nature of the client. The use of the term "client" in the ICF Core Competencies often represents an individual. The client in a team coaching context is a system, comprising multiple individuals (ICF, 2020).

CHAPTER 4

HOW TO READ THIS BOOK

"The meeting of two personalities is like the contact of two chemical substances: if there is any reaction, both are transformed."

– CARL JUNG

Relationships are complex, so this book is divided into three sections. The Basics will give you some of the critical terms and concepts you will need to introduce you to relationship systems work. For students of ORSC, there will also be some new terms, cases, and concepts. The Principles section will explore how systems behave and what they have in common. Part Three, Evolution Through Relationship, looks toward the next steps we need to take together to further evolve as a species.

Relationship Matters is a companion book to two other Relationship Systems books, *Creating Intelligent Teams* by Anne Rød and Marita Fridjhon and *Systems Inspired Leadership* by Frank Uit de Weerd and Marita Fridjhon. These powerful books apply systems work to professional and leadership fields. This book is written more for people on the street who would like to be more skillful at relationships at work and at home. As a reader, you may be a coach, consultant, leader, parent, spouse, or simply curious about what makes relationships tick.

This book is a blend of knowledge (information) and wisdom (experience), the objective and the subjective. We all learn differently. Some of us love data, and some of us love stories. To that end, the book includes the following components.

- **Research:** We will share some of the research that has helped to shape our thinking, particularly from psychology, process work, and organizational development fields.

- **Experience from the field:** CRR Global has over twenty years of experience working with teams, families, organizations, and community groups. We will present you with stories from our work and what we learned from the experience. Some of these stories will be personal, others professional.

- **Tools:** If we're going to get good at working with people, we're all going to need a tool kit. Scattered throughout the book are a few basic tools and skills to help with relationships. Please try them out.

- **Personal application:** Bring your own relationship experience to what you read and see what it has to offer you. This book is like a sourdough yeast starter. The starter culture is essential, but you must knead your own dough to make a rich loaf. We will give you some of the basic ingredients for creating great relationships. It will be up to you to bake the relationship bread. Use the book as a lens for your own relationships. Make it personal. Chew it over like any good sourdough bread.

To facilitate application, we have added Relationship Warrior questions and exercises in each chapter for you to apply to your own relationships.

This is where the learning will really start to stick. Practicing by doing, not just reading.

We can start with the question **what kind of relationship do you want to have with this book?** This question may seem strange. It's about being conscious and intentional about the kind of connection you want with this book. Maybe it's a casual fling. A committed relationship? Or even a one-night stand! It's up to you! But make sure that what you decide is a conscious choice. You picked up this book for a reason. What do you want to get out of it?

RELATIONSHIP WARRIORSHIP EXERCISE

- List two relationships you feel proud of. Be specific about who and why. What is it that makes you proud?

- List two relationships where you are struggling. Again, be specific about who and why. What do you wish could be different?

Use these relationships as lenses as you read this book to make it more personal and relevant for you.

PART 1
THE BASICS

CHAPTER 5

THE MODEL

In the last chapter, we introduced a model for the journey of this book. In this chapter, we will explore basic relationship terrain and visit some of the major stops along the way.

Let's start by breaking down the model for this book, which is split into three key elements: the mission, the path, and the goal.

MISSION

PATH

GOAL

EVOLUTION
THROUGH
RELATIONSHIP

RELATIONSHIP
WARRIORSHIP
(RELATIONSHIP
SYSTEM INTELLIGENCE)

RIGHT
RELATIONSHIP

THE MISSION – EVOLUTION THROUGH RELATIONSHIP

"**Evolution:** The gradual development of something, especially from a simple to a more complex form. A process of continuous change from a lower, simpler, or worse to a higher, more complex, or better state."

– OXFORD LANGUAGES

The process of evolving our relationships requires both **vertical** and **horizontal learning.**

Vertical learning is about personal development or the **being** aspect of who we are. It's about developing ourselves as people, deepening our wisdom, and exploring who we need to be in order to evolve our relationships. It's our own personal commitment to work on our relationships, our character, and our soul.

Horizontal evolution focuses on building skills, knowledge, and competencies, the **doing** aspects of relationship. It's about building skillful means in how we behave. For example, once we have a commitment to grow our relationships, we still need the skills and tools to express that growth. I may want to get along better with my son, but how do I actually do that? As a boss, how do I defuse this team conflict? Often, we know what needs to happen, but we're just not sure how to do it. Our desire for both vertical and horizontal evolution naturally leads us onto the path aspect of our model, Relationship Warriorship.

THE PATH – RELATIONSHIP WARRIORSHIP

"Only as a [spiritual] warrior can one withstand the path of knowledge. A warrior cannot complain or regret anything. His life is an endless challenge and challenges cannot possibly be good or bad. Challenges are simply challenges. The basic difference between an ordinary man and a warrior is that a warrior takes everything as a challenge, while an ordinary man takes everything as a blessing or a curse."

– DON JUAN, AS QUOTED BY JACK KORNFIELD IN *A PATH WITH HEART*

In chapter one, we said that if we do not evolve our capacity to live together in harmony with the planet and each other, we will not survive as a species. Relationship Warriorship is our path to do that. It is the vertical wisdom we need to develop our relationships. The path also includes the horizontal skills and tools, the Relationship Systems Intelligence, that gives us the doing aspect of relationship.

Relationship Warriorship is the heartfelt commitment to evolve and to learn through our connections with the world. **A Relationship Warrior is one who combats the universal enemy: self-ignorance.** It is the starting point, the inspiration that gives us the courage to walk the Right Relationship path even when it gets hard. Before we can master the "doing" aspect of relationship tools and skills, we need the heart to travel the path.

Reader, you may ask, *"Why do you use the word 'warriorship'? Isn't that awfully aggressive?"* The term Relationship Warriorship is adapted from Chögyam Trungpa's teachings, *Shambhala Warriorship: The Sacred Path of the Warrior*. It is about not turning away from our own character deficits but about bringing them into our awareness so we can work with them. As a Relationship Warrior, we work with our aggression by owning it, not marginalizing it.

Does this mean that we need to run out and take up arms or develop a warlike stance? Not at all. What we want to do is embody **the spirit** of a warrior. Spirit refers to that which gives life. Warriors live a life of action and clear direction. We can bring warrior spirit to the cause of harmonious connection because it is about life and living, not the use of power. Warrior spirit is a frame of mind that gives us courage and commitment.

Because, let's face it, nothing can get under our skin like the people we care about.

That's the power of relationships. When we are hurt, angry, and afraid, we need the fierce commitment to being warriors to stay the distance. **Relationship Warriorship means understanding that neither myself nor the other are the enemy. The enemy is ignorance.** Our commitment is to vanquish our own relationship ignorance over and over again. A true warrior is an ordinary being with commitment, a brave heart, and a genuine spirit. We are Relationship Warriors when we skillfully connect with others and bring all our wisdom and discernment.

We also use the term Relationship Warriorship because relationship isn't often at the forefront of our attention. We have not been taught to focus on relationship first, nor do our education systems or workplaces typically reward a relational focus. Our world favors the transactional over the relational, and we are rewarded for what we do, not how we relate.

Relationship Warriorship happens when you consider the relationship first. It is the courage to tell the truth to our boss, the heart to forgive our spouse, the confidence to leave a toxic relationship, and the wisdom to let go of control. We call it Relationship Warriorship because it involves taking a risk. Relationship Warriorship is not the path most often taken, but it's the one that is critical for our evolution towards Right Relationship. It gives us the attributes we need to walk the path of Right Relationship. These attributes include:

- **Bravery:** Relationship Warriors are fierce in their commitment to practice Right Relationship to the best of their ability. It takes courage to examine our gifts and our flaws in relating to others. Relationships are particularly scary because the people we care about have so much power over us. They can and do hurt us regularly. Our spouse leaves us; our kid is arrested; our work fires us; let's face it, relationships are a primary source of AFGOs (Another Fucking Growth Opportunity!) Sometimes, it takes all the courage we have to face the situation. Bravery is about falling down fourteen times and getting up fifteen. It is about **staying** in a difficult situation long enough to discern what is trying to happen.

- **Reducing our armor:** We think of warriors as being armored, but Relationship Warriors are brave enough to learn about and remove their armor when possible. Can we be brave enough to be vulnerable? Our armor may include our defenses, our stories about ourselves and others, our certainty, and our need to be right (the list goes on!).

Brené Brown talks about how our armor makes us feel safe, but it will not allow us to feel our world. Letting go of armor is not easy. Sometimes, the very thought of reducing my defensive armor makes me want to run for the exit. Every injury forces us to thicken our skin and to shore up our defenses. The problem is: with every increase in defenses, we are heavier, less able to move, and less able to feel. It is hard to dance when encased in armor. Relationship Warriors both honor and study their armor. How does it serve? What do I appreciate about it? How is it impeding my life? Can I adjust it or make it lighter? Am I willing to do that? Relationship Warriors are conscious and intentional about their armor. There are some situations where it is foolish to go without chain mail. Protect yourself! Other times, a bulletproof vest is just a habit that is getting in the way. Most of us don't want to be in bed with a suit of armor. The Relationship Warrior works to discern what armor is actually needed in service of Right Relationship.

- **Discipline:** Being a Relationship Warrior is a lifelong path and involves several aspects.

  - **Self-examination:** Am I willing to examine my contribution to the problem before pointing the finger at others? What part do I play in this issue? How am I co-responsible?

  - **Curiosity:** What does Relationship Warriorship mean in **this** situation, in **this** moment?

  - **Radical Responsibility:** Am I willing to practice the tools and skills that help me grow in relationship? Am I committed to my own growth and that of others? Examining our own responsibility for what is happening is so important that we have devoted part of a chapter to it.

- **Joy:** "*Wow, the above sounds like hard work. Why would I want to go through all that?*" The answer is to open up to joy! Relationships can be full of struggle and pain, but they are also our greatest source of joy. The more I practice Relationship Warriorship, the more joy I am open to receiving. The joy of being known, the joy of resolving a conflict, the joy of sharing a piece of pie, the joy of collaboration, the joy of a dew drop on a leaf. The joy of dancing with the world!

- **Lion's Roar:** Relationship Warriorship also helps us to develop something called the Lion's Roar.[8] Lion's Roar is unconditional confidence, the kind of confidence that is independent of circumstances. It is the trust in ourselves that we can find wisdom in whatever comes our way. No matter what happens, we can meet the situation directly and work with it. It is just the start of something trying to happen.

---

8   Lion's Roar is a metaphor used throughout Buddhist tradition to express fearlessness and confidence. As Tara Brach mentions in an article for *Psychology Today*, "It's the confidence that allows us to say, "No matter what life presents me, I can work with it." When that confidence is there, we take incredible joy in the moments of our lives. We are free to live life fully rather than resist and back off from a threat we perceive to be around the corner."

Lion's Roar is not based on a belief that "everything is going to be okay." It is based on the understanding that even when things are **not** okay, we can find a way to be with it. The situation has something to teach us. This, too, is a form of joy. What might be possible from here? If we really believed in Lion's Roar, how might we live our lives differently?

RELATIONSHIP SYSTEMS INTELLIGENCE – THE TOOLS OF RELATIONSHIP WARRIORSHIP

Relationship Warriorship gives us the courage to walk the path towards Right Relationship. But it is not enough. I may want to step into Right Relationship, but how do I do that when I am triggered by my boss or furious with my spouse? The Relationship Warrior needs the tools and skills of Relationship Systems Intelligence (RSI) to navigate the situation. RSI is the knowledge and craft of how to be skillful in any relationship circumstance. Relationship Warriorship inspires us, and Relationship Systems Intelligence (RSI) equips us. We will discuss it in depth in a later chapter, How Are You Intelligent.

The good news is that you are **already** practicing Relationship Warriorship. You are practicing it any time you:

- Say you are sorry
- Speak a difficult truth cleanly
- Hold the intensity of your feelings without acting them out unskillfully
- Ask for help
- Give up being "right"
- Examine your own responsibility before blaming another

We could go on and on listing many small and brave moments of Relationship Warriorship. The point we want to make is that you are already practicing Relationship Warriorship many times a day with the people you care about.

RELATIONSHIP WARRIORSHIP EXERCISE

Consider the following:

- Review the qualities we used above to describe Relationship Warriorship. Name three moments this week that you practiced Relationship Warriorship with yourself or with others.

- Name one moment this week where you **wish** you had practiced better Relationship Warriorship. What would you have done differently?

THE GOAL OF OUR JOURNEY – RIGHT RELATIONSHIP

MISSION	PATH	GOAL
EVOLUTION THROUGH RELATIONSHIP	RELATIONSHIP WARRIORSHIP (RELATIONSHIP SYSTEM INTELLIGENCE)	RIGHT RELATIONSHIP

The goal of our journey is Right Relationship, but what does that actually mean? People make up all kinds of stories about the term Right Relationship: *"If there is Right Relationship, is there Wrong Relationship? Is it about who gets to be right in an argument? Are we a far 'right' company in terms of political ideology?"*

So, what do we mean when we say Right Relationship?

Even after years of working with relationship systems, we still don't have an exact definition for Right Relationship. **Because Right Relationship will vary depending on the circumstances, and it will change from moment to moment.**

Definition of Right Relationship

"According to what is correct for a particular relationship situation. The best or most suitable of several possible behaviors for a particular relationship event."

– CRR GLOBAL

Generally speaking, Right Relationship is about bringing the best of yourself to any relationship situation that you encounter. And that, of course, begs the question: what **is** my best self, given the circumstances? Sometimes, bringing my best self means being generous, compassionate, and sensitive with the people we love. Other times Right Relationship means being raw, authentic, or confrontative, even if it's painful for someone to hear.

The key here is discernment. How do I discern what this situation needs? My teenage daughter comes home an hour late for curfew. She is distraught because her boyfriend just broke up with her. As a parent, does this situation need disciplinary action? Does it need empathy and kindness? The spouse of my employee receives a terminal diagnosis, and the employee starts missing a lot of work. As a boss, I am torn between good business practices and understanding. What do I do?

Right Relationship is something we can aspire to but never completely achieve. It is a commitment to being the best we can be with our families, teams, and community. It combines the commitment of Relationship Warriorship and the skills of Relationship Systems Intelligence.

To summarize the structures of this chapter:

- Relationship Evolution is **The Mission**

- Relationship Warriorship and Relationship Systems Intelligence are **The Path**

- Right Relationship is what we strive for, **The Goal**

Now that we have the map, the next section of this book will introduce you to some of the critical concepts of relationship systems: what they are, how they work, and the processes they follow.

CHAPTER 6

EVERYTHING IS RELATIONSHIP

"Beyond physics, relational thinking can be found in all the sciences. In biology, the characteristics of living systems are comprehensible in relation to their environment formed by other living beings. In chemistry, the properties of elements consist in the way in which they interact with other elements. In economics, we speak of economic relations. In psychology, the individual personality exists within a relational context. In this and many other cases, we understand things (organisms, chemicals, psychological life) through their being in relation to other things."

– CARLO ROVELLI, PHYSICIST; *HELGOLAND*

This book is called *Relationship Matters*, but what exactly do we mean by relationship? We hold a very broad view of that word.

"**Relationship:** the way in which two or more concepts, objects, or people are connected, or the state of being connected."

– OXFORD LANGUAGES

The most basic structures of the world involve relationship. Relationship is the primary driver of all things, from the tiny molecules that link our bodies together through chemical bonds, to the local galaxies swinging around each other in the web of gravity. All matter and energy are in a constant state of attraction, repulsion, or neutrality. The relationship between one thing and another is one of the most fundamental principles of the universe. We would like to explore the definition of what it means to be in relationship with someone or something. We have an ever-changing relationship with our bodies, our families, our work, our countries, our health, and our technology. We are connected to how we experience our coffee, our car, our computer, and ourselves.

> *"Each friend represents a world in us, a world possibly not born until they arrive, and it is only by this meeting that a new world is born."*
>
> – ANAIS NIN

 ## A STORY OF RELATIONSHIP

Your parents meet and are swept away by their mutual attraction. Their love for each other is consummated, and soon, you are conceived. In your mother's womb, you listen to her heartbeat until you are born. Later, childhood is full of an expanding circle of connections. You play and fight with your brothers and sisters and have a beloved stuffed animal.

At school, you love some teachers and loathe others, and you also learn about bullies and friends. It turns out you are good at soccer, and you train hard with your teammates. You bond with your soccer mates to eventually join a championship college team, greater than the sum of its parts. You fall in love and get your heart broken many times and learn painful lessons. You find you have a gift for science, and your teachers shape and encourage you to become a biologist. Since you love nature, you decide to specialize in researching climate change. At work, you are attracted to a particular colleague. The two of you date and are swept away by your connection. Your love for each other is consummated, and the next generation is born.

You build a house for your family, working with the architects and builders. You are frustrated with the solar power because it just doesn't work right. Your home is filled with friends and pets and kids. One day working in the yard, you notice that you are easily out of breath and have some chest pain. Your physician diagnoses you with heart disease and encourages you to change your diet and exercise more. But you hate exercise and miss your favorite foods. You are angry with your body as your heart disease gets worse, but you are also afraid of dying. You have many conversations with the universe or with God, sometimes angry, or bargaining, or denying. Eventually, you stop fighting your illness and gather the people you love close, and say goodbye to them in love and gratitude. You turn your face towards death, wondering what will happen next.[9]

Every single part of the above story is about connection and relationship. We are in relationship starting from the womb. Our circle of connection expands throughout our life, from family to friends, to colleagues, to our communities. Many of our relationship connections are with things or ideas. Things as varied as teddy bears, our profession, or even death. Each of these connections teaches us something about who we are, how we behave, and what we can expect.

---

9   The story reminded my editor, Katie, of the song "Wasn't Expecting That" by Jamie Lawson, which captures both the passing of time and the power of relationship. It's a lovely song if you've not heard it.

"But what if I'm a hermit and don't see anyone?" Some of us choose to limit our relationships, or we may just not like people much. Nevertheless, we are still always in relationship, particularly with ourselves. As we will discuss below, the first relationship system is ME. We are always in a complex relationship with our thoughts, feelings, and our bodies. Even if we lived completely alone, we are still in a complex dance with the world as we struggle with taxes, work, food, our worries, and our hopes. Relationship evolution is about understanding and navigating these connections better over time. We are shaped by our relationship experiences, and **every** experience is relational, whether with a concept, an object, a person, or a group. We don't know who we are without relationship to these things.

We hold that relationship includes ideas and objects in our lives. Our relationships with inanimate objects wax and wane and change, just as human relationships do. Relationships with objects have something to teach us about ourselves, especially if that object carries meaning for us.[10] Perhaps there is a day during your divorce when you finally take off your wedding ring. You have a powerful relationship with that slender golden band. It represents something important and is now being set aside. Similarly, for some people, the flag is a sacred object, not to be denigrated by being stepped on or burned. **Anything you have feelings for, you have a relationship with, whether a person, animal, idea, or a thing.**

From the boardroom to the bedroom, we believe *Relationship Matters*— because Relationship is fundamental to everything we do.

---

10 If you have ever wondered about the power of relationship to an inanimate object, try separating a five-year-old from his blankie!

CHAPTER 7

RELATIONSHIP SYSTEMS

The focus of this book will be on Relationship Systems. We call it "Relationship Systems" instead of just Relationships because the term Relationship Systems encourages the evolutionary shift to systems thinking. What makes ORSC evolutionary is its practical approach to Relationship Systems work. We know that relationships like to hang out together in systems, and we believe that systems thinking is the next evolutionary step for humankind. When we shift our lens from the individual to the systemic, an entirely new perspective opens up. Let's talk about what we mean by a Relationship System.

> "**Relationship Systems:** A Relationship System is a group of interdependent entities with a common focus or identity."
>
> — CRR GLOBAL

Notice that the definition says "entities," not "people," because not every relationship is with a single person or even with something animate. In an organization, the entity of the finance department has a relationship with the sales department, another entity. Each of these entities is its own systemic relationship collective. Also, relationship does not even depend on a living being. All of us are impacted by our thoughts and feelings about our dead mother, our money, or our health.

You'll notice that our definition of Relationship Systems also says interdependent. Interdependence is a key component of relationship systems. A group of strangers at the movies have a common focus: the movie. But most of the time, we're not interdependent at the movies. We're just a bunch of strangers, looking at the same screen and not interacting. However, when the kid behind you starts kicking your chair, your ability to enjoy the movie may become quite interdependent on your relationship with that child!

You may decide to say something to the kid. You might get involved with his parents. You may choose to move your seat. You and that family have become a short-term interactive Relationship System influencing one another. And certainly, if someone yells "**FIRE**," the audience will become interdependent quickly, as people either help or impede each other to an exit.

We are often in a complex interdependence with things as well as people or collectives. *"Hang on,"* you say . . . *"I'm dependent on money, but it's not dependent on me, so why are we interdependent?"* And that's certainly something to think about. How does your attitude, your expectations, or fears around money impact how you work with it? And how does money impact you back in terms of your life experiences? Your finances have a big impact on you! They influence what you can do and how you feel about yourself. If money were a person, how would you characterize your relationship with it? Would you call it a good relationship? Does it never call, never visit, never write? *"But wait,"* I hear you say, *"that relationship is imaginary. It's what I make up in my head. It's not real."*

Yes, that is true, and quite a lot of our relationship experience is dependent on what we make up in our heads. What are your political beliefs, and how do they influence your actions? Do you believe in God? Which God, and how does that impact your understanding of the world? Thoughts, beliefs, and ideas impact us![11] The story we make up in our heads shapes how we feel. And how we feel shapes our behaviors. How we behave is real. We have a relationship with everything that we impact, whether animate or inanimate. **If you feel something about it, you have a relationship with it.**

---

11 Thoughts, beliefs, and ideas are a part of the hidden forces that shape our reality. For example, we can see the clouds move, but we cannot see the wind. In the same way thoughts, beliefs and ideas can have an unconscious but powerful impact on how we behave in the world.

CHAPTER 8

LEVELS OF RELATIONSHIP

As we explore Relationship Systems, it is useful to have some maps and some common landmarks. Like any other discipline, relationships have deep structures, principles, and patterns. Understanding those patterns gives us the groundwork to understand how they work.

Relationships are multi-dimensional (that's why they are so complex!). They come in categories or holons.[12] Each level of a relationship is both a whole thing and a separate part of another relationship level. Systems are often nested within each other like Russian dolls. They function independently, but they also influence each other.

---

12 A "holon" is Greek for "whole/parts" meaning literally the whole that is simultaneously a part, and vice versa. The Greek word "holon" became popularized by Arthur Koestler's book, *The Ghost in the Machine* and Ken Wilber's, *A Brief History of Time*.

LEVEL 1: THE ME SYSTEM

"It is of practical value to learn to like yourself. Since you must spend so much time with yourself you might as well get some satisfaction out of the relationship."

— NORMAN VINCENT PEALE

ME

When we were small, we couldn't hold very much emotional intensity before proclaiming our discomfort. We were **hungry,** we were **wet,** we were **tired**. This responsiveness was natural and appropriate. It was our job to let the world know our needs so we could survive. As we got older and more socialized, we learned to contain our internal experiences. We became more conscious and intentional about how we might express ourselves in order to be more effective.[13]

---

13 There is much debate about whether this "socialization process" is a good thing or simply stunts the spirit. For the sake of this book, we are advocates for conscious and intentional behavior. We need to "feel what we feel" as important information, but we need to be at choice about how or if we respond to those feelings.

This is why the first relationship system is the self, or what we call the ME system. Most of us don't start out knowing that our "self," our character, is actually a system with its own interdependent entities. So, if you're wondering how on earth you can be a system of selves, just think about the last time you had an argument with yourself! Your mind is filled with different voices, different subpersonalities, each a part of who you are. Perhaps you are driving, and you come to an unfamiliar intersection in the road. One part of your mind is saying, "I think we should go left," and another part is saying, "I think we should go right," and you must pause to work out that little dilemma before you choose a direction. There are two different voices in your head with different opinions, and they disagree.

None of us are a single entity. Instead, we are more like a cut gemstone. We are one single, beautiful gem of a person, but with multiple facets. As we move through our day, different facets of our character pop up—perhaps the side of me that's hopeful, the side of me that's jealous, or a side of me that's uncertain. All these dozens of facets make up the entity of who we are. So, every person is an integrated self (the gemstone we think of as ME), but we have multiple facets of self that make us flexible and give us range. This is true for everyone and is entirely normal.[14]

GEM

14 Sometimes people ask, "*Do you mean we all have dissociative disorders, with multiple personalities?*" As a psychologist, I would say **yes** and **no**. All people have many different aspects of self that we think of as ME. However, the boundaries are fluid between these different aspects, so we shift smoothly between them. People with dissociative disorders tend to be more compartmentalized; their aspects are more siloed and sometimes out of touch with one another. Dissociative people often develop a brilliant strategy to wall off parts of themselves, to protect themselves from unbearable experiences. All people do this to a certain degree but our boundaries between our selves are usually more blended than that of people with dissociative disorder.

A question we're often asked about the ME system is: *"How do all those parts get along with each other?"* Well, we are always in relationship with our different aspects, and like any relationship, some days are better than others! Sometimes we go into therapy or coaching because our internal "selves" do not get along well with each other. There may be big conflicts between different parts of ourselves that need to be resolved if we are going to have any peace of mind. Other times we come together as a smoothly functioning entity, or we shift effortlessly from one iteration of self to another.

When our ME system functions fairly smoothly, this can be called emotional intelligence, or EQ. EQ is the ability to know, understand, and articulate the different aspects of ourselves. And let's have some compassion for ourselves. It's not always easy getting this motley crew of 'selves' together. We will talk about this more in the Intelligences chapter.

LEVEL 2: YOU/ME (DYAD RELATIONSHIP SYSTEMS)

> *"You can kiss your family and friends good-bye and put miles between you, but at the same time, you carry them with you in your heart, your mind, your stomach, because you do not just live in a world, but a world lives in you."*
>
> – FREDERICK BUECHNER

The next level of relationship systems is the pairs level, or what we call the YOU/ME system. YOU/ME systems bring yourself and another together. They can be intimate, as in a relationship with our spouse or child. They can also be professional—our relationship with a manager or colleague. Any paired relationship is a YOU/ME relationship.[15]

---

15 In ORSC courses, YOU/ME holons are called WE. It is changed in this book to differentiate it clearly from the WE of the larger collective systems.

YOU - ME

One way to think about this is that the ME system of myself and the ME system of yourself come together in the YOU/ME relationship of the two of us. And that can make things complicated because everything becomes a group process! If I think about my relationship with Marita, I know that I absolutely adore 85 percent of Marita's different selves. And then I can tolerate about 10 percent of Marita—I'm not crazy about those parts of her, but I can live with them. Finally, there's about 5 percent of Marita's selves that totally get on my nerves! My collection of internal selves just doesn't get along with that 5 percent of her selves. This is actually a pretty fantastic relationship ratio! If you mostly love 85 percent of your partner, you're in good shape. And, of course, it fluctuates day to day. Also, don't forget, Marita has her own set of percentages when she considers her relationship to my different selves. Relationship is a mixed bag. Your loving wife still has parts of her that are driven crazy by your obsession with golf. You love your daughter but hate the part of her that got a tattoo. Having mixed feelings about parts of the people we love is part of the relationship territory.

This happens at work as well. There are many parts of ourselves interacting with many parts of our colleagues. We all know that when we hire someone new, we are full of positive expectations. As we get to know them over time, we learn more and more that they, too, have their difficulties and problems, as well as their unexpected talents! We learn this by spending time together in the YOU/ME relationship. These systems are a primary way we grow because they are often intense and push our buttons. We may not be aware of many aspects of self until we discover them with a partner.

It is also fair to assume that each relationship will uncover new aspects of self. I may not know that I have a jealous self until my lover pays attention to a possible rival. **Relationships reveal me to myself**. I cannot know who I am until my friend/child/boss reveals some new aspect of myself. Relationships are the path of self-awareness, sometimes called the "difficult yoga." Almost all our experiences, good and bad, arise because of our relationship to something: losing a valuable piece of jewelry, being swept away by a new idea, having a crush on someone, or struggling with a migraine. This is the tapestry of experience that is mediated by another person, object, or experience we are connecting to. We do not know who we are until we are in relationship.

LEVEL 3: WE (COLLECTIVE RELATIONSHIP SYSTEMS)

*"Everything that irritates us about others can
lead us to an understanding of ourselves."*

– CARL JUNG

Finally, there are larger systemic entities that we relate to on a daily basis. Once we move past the YOU/ME, we are in the larger collective relationship systems of WE.[16] This involves larger groups of people, so the WE

---

16 In ORSC courses, this relationship systems holon is called IT.

WE SYSTEM

could be a team, a department, your extended family, your country, or nature. All of them will push you to evolve.

It has always bugged me that there are so many stories about people retreating away in caves to get enlightened! It's easy to get enlightened all alone in a cave because there's no one there to irritate you. If you want to get enlightened, try living in a small apartment with a large family during a pandemic! Be a Relationship Warrior when your spouse is down with a cold, your teenager dents the car, and your four-year-old has stuffed a marble up his nose. When you can deal with anything that a WE relationship can throw at you, **that's Right Relationship.**

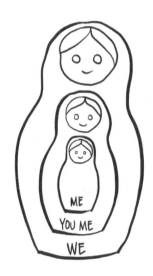

Relationship systems tend to nest within each other like Russian dolls.

Every collective WE system probably has at least one YOU/ME in it. For example, your relationship with your spouse is nested within your family system. This is also true for organizational systems. The boss (ME) is enfolded into a different relationship with everyone on the management team (YOU/ME), as well as with the management team as a collective (WE).

Clearly, relationship systems are linked. Connections increase in complexity, as the relationship levels interact and influence one another. And yet, none of us get any training in relationship (outside of "clean up after yourself" in kindergarten!).

CHAPTER 9
THE THIRD ENTITY

"The Third Body"

A man and a woman sit near each other, and
they do not long at this moment to be older, or younger,
nor born in any other nation, or time, or place.
They are content to be where they are,
talking or not talking.
Their breaths together feed someone we do not know.
The man sees the way his fingers move;
he sees her hands close around a book she hands to him.
They obey a third body they have in common.
They have made a promise to that body.
Age may come, parting may come, death will come.
A man and a woman sit near each other;
as they breathe they feed someone we do not know,
someone we know of, whom we have never seen.

– ROBERT BLY

There are lots of different things going on at the ME level, the YOU/ME level, and the WE level all at the same time. The good news is that regardless of the size of the relationship system you are working with, **all relationship systems have one thing in common, the Third Entity.** And the Third Entity is a wonderfully simplifying principle. All Relationship Systems, at any level, have a Third Entity. In fact, the "Third Entity" is another name for the Relationship System itself.

"**Third Entity:** Along with the ME, YOU/ME and WE of the relationship, there is a third thing, the relationship itself, as if it were its own living, breathing entity. This Third Entity has its own wisdom and knowledge that we can tap into."

– CRR GLOBAL

Whenever two or more people come together, there will always be a Third Entity, the Relationship System. This Third Entity is not one person or another but is a combination of every person and is greater than any individual. It's the Third Entity concept that sets the ORSC approach apart. There are other kinds of systems coaching approaches, but to our knowledge, we're the only ones that hold the Third Entity as a critical concept for working effectively with relationships.

Most of us understand the concept of a Relationship System, but how do we work with it? **We can learn how to see, to hear, to sense the Third Entity,** in order to work directly with its wisdom. *"Is there something tangible and physical there that can be objectively measured as the Third Entity?"* No, there isn't. But there are many invisible things that we hold as real, such as love, God, hope, etc. The Third Entity is a useful concept that can help us access relationship wisdom and perspective. Mathematics has the concept of an "imaginary number," which is the square root of negative one. The square root of negative one is an impossible construct used to bring new knowledge and a fresh perspective to mathematics.[17] In the same way, the Third Entity perspective brings fresh information to relationship issues. We cannot lay our hands on a Third Entity, but we can and do learn to see it, hear it, and sense it. So, how does the Third Entity fit into our model for the book introduced in chapter one?

THE THIRD ENTITY AND RELATIONSHIP EVOLUTION

Working with the Third Entity is evolutionary because it immediately shifts our perspective to systemic thinking.[18] It gives us a more comprehensive, connected, and expansive view of things, allowing us to see the relationship forest as well as the trees. Systemic thinking involves a perceptual shift from seeing individuals to seeing the interactions between them.

The Third Entity supports walking **the Path** of our model, Relationship Warriorship, and particularly Relationship Systems Intelligence. The Third Entity helps us to connect with the integrated whole, the gemstone of a system. By pulling all the facets of the system into one entity, we gain a practical tool that helps us access the wisdom of the system. We can access it in the tools below to learn what the system feels and wants. In turn, the metaview of the Third Entity develops Relationship Warriorship by helping us move past our small subjective experience to the broader perspective of the relationship itself. It's a way to step out of your own shoes or story for a moment and see the bigger picture.

---

17 Imaginary numbers, also called complex numbers, are used in real-life applications such as electrics and quadratic equations. An imaginary number is a real number multiplied by the imaginary unit i, which is defined by its property $i^2 = -1$. By definition, it is considered to be both real and imaginary. Like other immeasurable concepts, including love and your emotions!

18 Adult developmental theory lists systemic thinking as a highly developed understanding of the world.

Finally, the Third Entity also helps us connect with our goal of Right Relationship. Like those nested dolls, it provides a metaview of the relationship system that incorporates the concerns of the ME, the YOU/ME, and the WE. When we stand in the Third Entity, we do not take sides; we can recognize that all the voices of the system carry important information. A systems thinker is someone who embraces the idea that the whole is greater than the sum of its parts.

We have been living with the Third Entity our whole lives. Many animals instinctively connect with collective systemic awareness. We feel a sense of wonder when we watch a murmuration of hundreds of starlings wheeling through the sky together. How do they not knock into one another? How do schools of sardines turn on a dime together? Clearly, they are not moving as individuals; they are instinctively attuned to the Third Entity of the swarm and can move as one. As human beings, many of us are already doing this instinctively, especially with larger groups.

You are giving a speech at a large convention. When you walk out onto the stage, there are 500 strangers there. You cannot relate to 500 people. Instead, your senses start working to connect with the whole, with the Third Entity, the audience. You start getting information from seeing them. Are they still? Are people milling about? Are people leaving? Absorbing the sight of the Third Entity, perhaps you give people a moment to find a seat.

As you give your speech, you hear the Third Entity: Is there a big murmur because of something you say? Are people suddenly silent? You start trying to figure out what that silence might mean.

You are sensing the Third Entity: What is the emotional field in the room? Do people seem excited, anxious, confused? Do you feel connected to them? Every one of your senses is instinctively reaching out to the Third Entity of *the group and garnering information. You do this naturally. You know that great speakers have the ability **to connect with the audience**. This is another phrase for synching with the Third Entity.*

Sports teams are another natural way to experience the Third Entity. There are quite a few movies about the magical moment when a team moves past the individual players to move as a single integrated whole. They are moving like a flock of birds or a school of fish. They are connected to one body, the team's Third Entity.

When we work with smaller systems, it can be easy to get distracted by the individuals. For example, when I am interacting with a couple, it is easy for me to ping-pong my focus between one person and the other. Maybe I like the wife better, so I find my allegiance is subtly shifting in her direction. I am starting to take sides. But from the Relationship Systems perspective, the client to be served is neither the husband nor the wife. The client I have been hired to serve is the Third Entity, the relationship **between** the couple. Learning to work from the Third Entity allows us to shift our perception of relationships from individuals to the relationship between them. We have made the evolutionary shift to a systemic view.

The path to developing Relationship Systems Intelligence is learning to see, hear, and feel the Third Entity. This chapter will give you some tools to connect to the Third Entity of the ME, YOU/ME, and WE systems.

THE THIRD ENTITY OF ME

Remember the gemstone? You, the reader, are a Third Entity of selves, a collective gem of all the different aspects of yourself. So, within the system of Faith, there are different facets: many selves with different characters or roles. But ultimately, there is one thing, one Faith. How I

ME

express myself may vary by which subpersonality facet is operational, but the Third Entity of Faith is the gemstone holding all those parts. Faith is the relationship matrix, the Third Entity, within which my many "selves" exist. *"Okay, but which self is true?"* All of them are true in the sense that every voice is authentic in the moment. My irritation with an employee who fails to show up is real. When I hear he had a car accident and is in the hospital, my reaction naturally switches to one of compassion for the colleague. Both experiences are experientially true. As I evolve my Relationship Warriorship, I also evolve my ability to hold more emotional complexity without impulsively acting out from just one facet of myself. As I grow and change over the years, the different facets of myself will change also. Some facets of ME may subside. For example, as I retire, the part of myself that is the President of CRR Global is receding. Other facets of my Third Entity will grow or be added, like Faith the Author. Yet the Third Entity of "Faith," the gemstone, will remain recognizable and familiar to those who know me. The components of Faith can and must change, but the Third Entity of Faith will remain.

RELATIONSHIP TOOL: PAPER CONSTELLATION OF THE ME SYSTEM

The system map below allows us to **see** the different facets of the Third Entity of ME. It is one form of the Paper Constellation tool we use with systems. Below is an example of how the exercise works.[19]

Let's imagine that I just got a big promotion at work. I am excited, but I also have a lot of other feelings about it. I will use the Paper Constellation to map out all the different selves that are operating within my ME system. By putting them out on paper, I can explore my different feelings and increase my self-awareness. One self in me feels excited about the promotion, my **Excited Self**. Another, **Anxious Self**, has performance anxiety. "Will I be able to measure up to the new job?" There is an

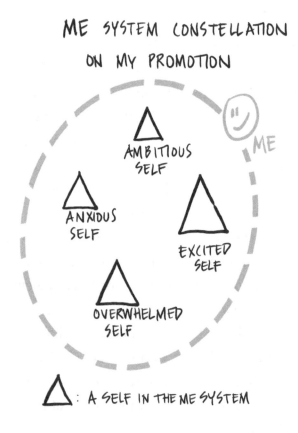

ME SYSTEM CONSTELLATION
ON MY PROMOTION

AMBITIOUS SELF

ME

ANXIOUS SELF

EXCITED SELF

OVERWHELMED SELF

△ : A SELF IN THE ME SYSTEM

19 ORSC students feel free to use the more complex form of constellations taught in the Geography course.

Ambitious Self, which is already starting to think about the next step in my career. Finally, there is an **Overwhelmed Self**, struggling to deal with all the changes. These are the major **Selves** operating in my ME system around my promotion.

The ME system Paper Constellation increases my emotional intelligence about my reaction to my promotion. For example, I notice that the largest self is the Excited Self. I drew it largest because that self carries my primary emotion. Also, each of these selves influences one another. Both my Anxious Self and Overwhelmed Self reinforce my discomfort about the change. My Ambitions Self and Excited Self strengthen positive feelings about the promotion. The relationships between the different Selves pull on the ME Third Entity.

Now, it is time for you to give it a try. Pick a topic that you have some conflicting feelings about.

RELATIONSHIP WARRIORSHIP EXERCISE

1. Draw a big circle on a piece of paper—this represents your ME system Third Entity. Write down the topic you will explore at the top of the page.

2. Identify and place all your different selves in your ME system inside the circle. Put names on each self so you know what each is feeling. You might make some selves bigger than others in terms of their influence. Feel free to be creative about how you draw the different selves if you like. There isn't a right way to draw this.

3. Step back and have a look at your constellation. The constellation exercise is a way to articulate your many aspects to see the

factors creating it. Reader, what else do **you** notice about your constellation?

4. Think about the relationships between the different selves. Which selves reinforce each other, and which ones might be conflictual? How are their relationships impacting your ME Third Entity? Is there anything you would like to change or add moving into your future? How might you do that?

The ME Third Entity Constellation helps us get clear about the complex feelings we may have about a situation.

THE THIRD ENTITY OF YOU/ME

YOU - ME

Since every relationship system has a Third Entity, we can connect with the Third Entity of any YOU/ME system as well. We can think about the Third Entity of any relationship as if it were a living, breathing, alive thing. There is a Third Entity of your relationship with your spouse, with your child, and one between you and your health. The Third Entity is the creative union of both members of the relationship.

The Third Entity also references your relationship with inanimate objects. So, at this moment, you are in a relationship with an object, this book. In the Reader/Book system, the ME is the person reading this book— and the YOU is the book itself. And therefore, there is also a third thing, the relationship between yourself and the book. The book will interact with you by provoking experiences within you. You might love certain parts; other parts may feel annoying. But there is a creative act happening between the two of you. Your feelings, insights, and irritations are arising within your Third Entity with the book. This call-and-response creative act can't happen without the book, and it can't happen without you; they are interdependent. Artists know creation is a collaborative venture between the métier and the creator.

The Third Entity can offer us wisdom that can shape how we are together in relationship. We can contact it at any time. Let's walk together through the different parts of a YOU/ME system and see what it has to teach us.

Start by thinking of a relationship that is important to you, but that has a small conflict or a hot spot. It can be a personal relationship like a family member, or a work relationship you truly care about. Imagine a triangle in the space that you are in, and each corner has one voice of the conflict. You are going to walk through the different imaginary perspectives of each of the entities in this scenario, the ME, the YOU/ME, and the Third Entity. As you walk through the different voices of the system, let yourself be in touch with your feelings and intuition more than your intellect. Let your heart inform you.

RELATIONSHIP WARRIORSHIP EXERCISE: THE THIRD ENTITY – HEARING THE THIRD ENTITY OF YOU/ME.

First, we want to understand the individual voices in the system. Both YOU and ME have their own perspectives on the difficulty. This exercise is most powerful when you physically walk back and forth between the positions you are inhabiting. This will help you to clarify the feelings of the voice you are expressing.

Start out by standing in the ME position of the reader in the graphic above. Imagine that you can see the other person, the YOU, standing across from you. Begin by firmly standing in the ME, and across from you is the person with whom you are having a conflict (YOU).

This is your chance to tell that person what **you feel** and what **you want** from your side of the conflict. Be honest about what you say; you are developing your EQ by getting in touch with the ME system.

When you have gotten clear about your ME opinion, it is time to step into the shoes of the person opposite you (YOU). To do this, you need to drop your side of the story enough to feel your way into YOU's experience of the conflict. That person has their own feelings and desires around the issue. Walk into the YOU position and let yourself empathize with their side of the story. What would YOU respond back to ME about what **they feel and want**? This step is developing social intelligence, the ability to understand another person's point of view. Yes, you are **imagining** what they feel and want, but you probably know at least something about that. If you truly have no idea what they feel and want, that is also useful information. Would you like to find out from them in real life? It is often helpful to step back and forth between the ME corner and the YOU corner and develop a dialogue, until both positions are clear. The clearer the ME and YOU voices are, the easier it is to find the perspective of the Third Entity.

The final corner of the triangle to explore is the Third Entity position. When you step there, you allow yourself to feel into **being the Relationship itself, as if it were a separate, breathing, living entity with its own perspective and wisdom on the problem**. Finding the voice of the Third Entity is a new experience for most of us. We usually know how the ME feels about something, and we often know the other person's view (the YOU). But now, we want to step into the relationship's perspective. As the Third Entity watches the ME and the YOU struggling with this disagreement, **how does it feel about those two people**? After all, those people belong to the relationship!

What is it experiencing as it watches them in this conflict? Does it feel sad, concerned, or hopeful for them? The Third Entity has its own wisdom we can tap into. **If it knew something that the other two people didn't know, what would it say to them? What does the relationship need from those two people that might be helpful?** The Third Entity's voice helps us get in touch with the voice of the system. The path of Relationship Warriorship is about developing our understanding of ourselves, others, and the needs of the system itself, the Third Entity.

THE THIRD ENTITY OF WE

Of course, larger systems like teams, families, and organizations have their own Third Entity as well. There is the gemstone that represents the entity of the company, but there are also multiple departments that are

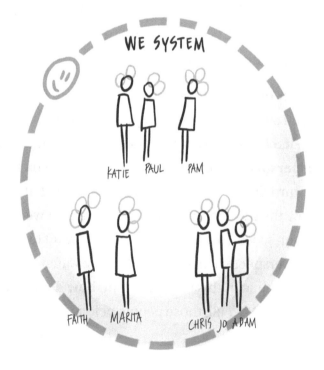

like the facets of that company. Every departmental facet has its own composite character and its own wisdom to share. Teams and families are similar. There will be multiple members within a single team, but that team itself will have its own "personality" or Third Entity that will be distinct from other teams. By contacting the Third Entity of a system, we can obtain its wisdom and perspective.

RELATIONSHIP WARRIORSHIP EXERCISE: MEETING THE ORGANIZATIONAL THIRD ENTITY

Just as we worked with the Third Entity of the YOU/ME system, we can also harvest the wisdom of an organizational or departmental Third Entity. Let's imagine I want to hear from the wisdom of the Finance Department. This department has its own Third Entity encapsulated within the larger organizational Third Entity.

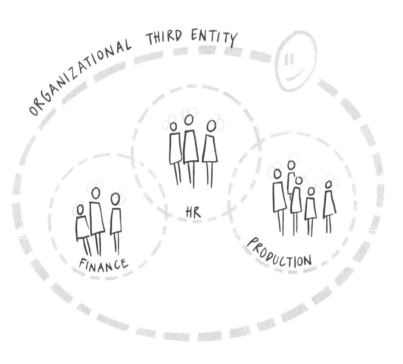

In this exercise, I will be moving back and forth between my own voice (ME) and the voice of the Finance Department (WE) as I imagine it.

1. ME speaking to WE

It's always helpful to start with appreciation. I begin by telling the Finance Department what gifts it brings to myself or to the company. I know this system well, and there are many things I can **appreciate** about it. All relationships have good and bad aspects to them. When I have completed my appreciation, I will next tell the Finance Department the **challenges** it poses to me or to the company. Finally, as ME, I will tell Finance what I **need** from it.

2. WE speaking to ME

However, this is a partnership. The Finance Department (WE) has its own things it may need to say to Faith (ME). Imagine what it wants to speak to ME. What does it appreciate about Faith? What challenges does she pose to the department? What does Finance need from Faith? Imagine what it would be like to step back and forth and have a spirited conversation with this department.

3. Speaking from the Third Entity

Now that there has been an honest exchange, the ME (Faith) and WE (Finance) can join in the Third Entity of the relationship. If Faith takes hands with the Finance Department, what does our partnership want to be in the world together? What is the vision/mission of our Third Entity? How can we support one another?

Now, it is your turn to try it. Begin by selecting a WE system that you would like to know more about. It can be a team, a department, a family, or an organization, as long as it is a system that you care about. Use an image to represent that WE system and place it somewhere apart from you so you can see it as separate from you. Using your imagination, what does the image of that WE system look like? Make it real. How would it move, talk, etc.? Get a good sense of the WE character. Now, you can have a conversation with your system using the above steps.

Reader, notice what is different for you as a result of doing this exercise. What did you learn? Did you get stuck anywhere? Is there an action step you might want to take because of this exercise? The action step could be something simple, such as telling people about your experience of the exercise.

SENSING THE SYSTEM

Along with **seeing the system** and **hearing** the system, it is important to learn to **sense** the system. The WE exercise above is one way we learn to sense the system and make it an ally to our understanding. There are other useful skills for sensing the system. Every interaction has what we call an emotional field that we can feel. All systems have emotional "weather" that we experience. The emotional field is the complex, ever-shifting flow of feelings that is generated through relationship. The emotional field ebbs and flows and changes like smoke within a system.

In a large group, there may be several emotional fields as different subgroups experience different things. This is not a new idea; we have already been sensing this from a very young age. We feel the emotional field much of the time. We just rarely talk about it. Helping a relationship system to sense, acknowledge, and label its emotional field is a very useful tool for revealing what is going on in a situation. We call this reading the emotional field. Here are some examples that you have probably already experienced.

- You walk into a conference room where you can immediately tell that there has been a fight. You can sense the tension.

- Your spouse comes home, and before they even come into the kitchen to greet you, you can tell they had a bad day. There are subtle cues about the sound of putting their briefcase down, the length of time it takes them to come to see you, and whether they shouted out a greeting.

- Your teenager is mad at you and your spouse. They don't have to say a word; the atmosphere simmers with resentment during dinner. (Teenagers are masters of creating emotional fields.)

- You go on a blind date, and something about your partner makes you uncomfortable. You can't put your finger on it, but your "creep factor" alarm goes off.

The emotional field is something we are sensing with our spidey senses all day long, but we often ignore it. We detect it through a combination of subtle sensory cues and pattern recognition that we may not even be aware of. The military calls this "intuition" and has studied it as a critical leadership skill.[20]

---

20 In 2014, the Office of Naval Research embarked on a four-year, $3.85 million research program to explore and understand the use of intuitive decision-making, or what I've called "spidey senses." The aim of the program was to better understand this so-called "sixth sense" in order to capitalize on and spread the power of intuition throughout the military.

As relational human beings, we naturally feel the emotional field that is moving through a situation. However, we often ignore it or are unconscious of it. At CRR Global, we teach students to read the emotional field (EF). This very simple tool involves noticing and labeling the emotional field that is in the room and is useful for several reasons:

- It helps the people in the system to also notice and be conscious of the emotional field that is swirling around in the room. We cannot address something until we have recognized and acknowledged it.

- It increases the emotional, social, and Relationship Systems Intelligence of the system. It does this by helping people recognize and name the feelings that they are having but may not have expressed.

- Acknowledging a feeling that is in the room often brings a sense of relief. The elephant in the room is finally being spoken to. Then, the system has options about how to work with the situation.

Reading the emotional field helps to normalize emotions, especially in professional groups. Emotions are the natural currency of relationship. When we co-create feelings together—exchanging them or reacting to them—we enter a creative space where we are influencing one another. Some kind of emotional field *is always there*. Certain emotional fields are touching, scary, or flat. Some feel refreshingly honest or stink like dead fish. Emotional fields are not good or bad; they are information we can tap into and use.

You don't have to get it right to read the emotional field. One time, I was working with a business partnership on a delicate topic. One partner had provided most of the financing for the company, and the other partner was negotiating "sweat equity." They were laughing about the situation, and I read the emotional field: "I love the humor. It's great that you are laughing about this." One partner looked up and said with a chuckle, "Oh no, this is nervous laughter." I had read the emotional field wrong, but in the process of correcting me, the actual emotional field was revealed. You also do not have to label the field if you are not sure. Sometimes, you can say, "Something just happened here, but I'm not sure what it was. What do you think it was?" Or you can just ask, "What's in the emotional field right now?" And let them tell you. Most people are comfortable with the term emotional field. They instinctively understand what it means.

RELATIONSHIP WARRIORSHIP EXERCISE: READING THE EMOTIONAL FIELD

As we mentioned above, you already know how to sense the emotional field. However, most of us have gotten out of the habit of speaking to it out loud. Below is a great way to increase your awareness and facility with reading the emotional field.

- Stream one of your favorite television shows. Set a timer for every fifteen minutes. When the timer goes off, pause your program, and read the emotional field that is happening on the screen. There may be several happening at the same time. Don't worry about getting it right. The exercise will develop your ability to notice the emotional field and get more fluid about putting it into words.

- In real life, when you're talking with your team or family, if you aren't clear about the emotional field, you can just ask about it: "What's going on between you two right now?"

- Notice if some kinds of emotional fields are easier or more difficult for you to express. Don't judge; just notice.

BENEFITS OF WORKING FROM THE THIRD ENTITY

So, we have looked at three ways of detecting the Third Entity of a system; seeing it, hearing it, and sensing it. Each of these approaches helps us to open our awareness to the system as an entity.

Let's review some of the reasons why working with the Third Entity can make our life easier and help us to evolve:

- **The Third Entity simplifies things.** In the previous sections, we looked at the complexities of systems. There are holonic levels (ME, YOU/ME, WE). There are multiple parts of me interacting with multiple parts of you; it all feels complicated. The Third Entity helps us to shift our perception from individuals to the systemic whole. Instead of needing to work with all fifteen people in our community group, we only need to work with one thing, the Third Entity of that system. The unique individuals of these systems (the fifteen people) are still there, but they are also folded into one thing, the Third Entity. We are engaged with the relationship between them.

- **We can access the wisdom of the system.** We can step outside of our individual perspective to connect imaginatively with the Third Entity, as we did in the exercises above. *"Wait a minute,"* I hear you say, *"aren't I just making up what the Third Entity would say? Aren't I just talking with myself?"* To a certain degree, yes. Sometimes our ego is so bound up with what is happening with our family or team that it is hard to be a clear channel to accurately hear another's experience. But from the systemic perspective, **we are not separate from our team, spouse, or company.** We are part of it, so we also have access to what the collective knows. The voice of the Third Entity often offers a metaview, a fresh perspective that we cannot quite access as an individual. If you step into the voice of the Third Entity and it is exactly the same as your personal opinion, chances are **you haven't really**

connected with the Third Entity. Sometimes, we do Third Entity work with teams that have a disagreement about how to address an issue. We place a chair in the middle of the team circle, the Third Entity Chair. We ask the team members to come and sit in the chair, go inside, and get in touch with what the team's Third Entity feels about the situation. Instructions include, "When you come to sit in the Third Entity chair, be sure to leave your own tightly held personal opinion in your own seat. If you already know what the Third Entity would say, then it probably is your own opinion, **not** the voice of the Third Entity. When you sit in the chair, do your best to empty out and wait to see what the Third Entity wants to say."

● **We evolve our spidey senses.** When we begin to relate to the voice of the system, we start to develop new ways to work with it. The Paper Constellation teaches me **to see** all the parts of the ME system. The YOU/ME Third Entity Exercise teaches me **to hear** the different voices of the pair system: my voice, my partner's voice, and the voice of the Third Entity. Reading the emotional field teaches me **to sense** the system.

Once we can see, hear, and sense systems, we start to find them everywhere! Different systems link together, like the mycelium network under the soil. Suddenly we can observe that the fiscally conservative finance department is exerting a natural control over the spending exuberance of the R&D department. We can sense how one aggressive manager is diminishing the creativity of the whole advertising team.

Thinking systemically is a paradigm shift that both broadens our awareness and gives us a new way to perceive the world. We can still see the trees, but suddenly, we can see, hear, and feel the forest. How big of a system can I hold? How much of the systemic world am I willing to identify with: my family, the country, the natural world? The size of a system we are willing to identify with is very personal. Systemic awareness expands our world and stretches our identity. On the one hand, I evolve as I become an integral part of ever-larger systems. At the same time, experiencing the complexities of all the parts of the system can feel confusing. As my empathy expands, my certainty about "what is right" becomes more diffuse. Holding multiple viewpoints can stretch our viewpoint to what may feel like a breaking point. It takes time and Relationship Warriorship to grow into our larger perspectives.

CHAPTER 10

HOW ARE YOU INTELLIGENT?

Relationship Systems generate a lot of emotional fields; indeed, emotions are often what we exchange to connect with one another. If we want to evolve as a species, we need to become more capable of managing that exchange. We want to spend the next few pages talking about the different types of relationship intelligences since they are the foundations for creating good relationships.

In the last section, we mentioned emotional intelligence (EQ) and social intelligence (SI) as a basis by which we navigate ME and YOU/ME systems. In this section, we will also discuss Relationship Systems Intelligence (RSI) as a core aspect of understanding WE systems. Each intelligence is about developing expanding circles of awareness about relationships with self, others, and larger collectives. Our emotional intelligence allows us to identify what we are feeling and to choose the best way to express it. Our social intelligence allows us to empathize with and understand the emotions of another. Relationship Systems Intelligence allows us to be with, witness, and support the interactions of any kind of system, including the ME and YOU/ME systems. EQ and SI have been around for a long time. They are the street smarts of relationship. This chapter will make them less theoretical and more practical as the building blocks to the next intelligence, Relationship Systems Intelligence.

EMOTIONAL INTELLIGENCE (EQ)

We all know the emotional fields we struggle with inside. If I feel attacked by someone, it is natural to become triggered and drop into a reactive emotional hole. I may become defensive, counterattack, or freeze like a deer in headlights. My ability to consciously respond to what is happening is instantly diminished. Instead, I am trapped and looping in my internal narrative. This is normal and happens to all of us. And, as we mature and work on ourselves, we are better able to stand in the confidence of Lion's Roar. Our emotional container expands as we develop Relationship Warriorship. This doesn't mean that we stop reacting to things. It means we have greater degrees of freedom about **how** we react to things. We become more conscious and intentional about how we respond to the situation.

Daniel Goleman[21] has spent the last thirty years establishing the importance of emotional intelligence in the workplace, specifically in business leadership. In one of *Harvard Business Review's* most well-read articles, "What makes a leader," Goleman argues that: "The most effective leaders are alike in one crucial way: They all have a high degree of what has come to be known as emotional intelligence. It's not that IQ and technical skills are irrelevant. They do matter, but mainly as 'threshold capabilities'; that is, they are the entry-level requirements for executive positions. But my

---

21 Daniel Goleman is perhaps best known for his 1995 text, "Emotional Intelligence." We'd highly recommend that classic text alongside, "Primal Leadership: realizing the power of emotional intelligence" and "Focus: The hidden drive of excellence."

research, along with other recent studies, clearly shows that emotional intelligence is the 'sine qua non' of leadership. Without it, a person can have the best training in the world, an incisive, analytical mind, and an endless supply of smart ideas, but he still won't make a great leader" (2004).

Since the first system is ME, my relationship skills must first begin with myself. Do I understand what is happening inside me, my motivations, reactions, and emotions? When we are born, we are given a fantastic instrument, including a body, mind, and soul. But like any instrument, it doesn't do us much good until we learn to play it. Emotional intelligence helps us to understand the kind of instrument we are. As a musical instrument, each of us has a unique range of emotional expression. At any moment, are you a drum set, strong and bold, critical to holding the structure of the music? Are you a harp, ethereal, and technically complex? Most of us are **many** instruments, expressing a huge range. But before we can create music with others, we need to know how to play our own instrument. Learning our own instrument is what emotional intelligence is all about. And it is a lifelong journey.

Emotional intelligence (EQ): CRR Global defines emotional intelligence as "the ability to experience, identify, interpret, express, and skillfully employ emotions."

Experiencing My Emotions

So, how do we go about developing our EQ? Let's break down the above definition. Some of us are very in touch with our emotions. But the way in which we experience them varies widely. Emotions are experienced in the body. It takes time to learn that my tense stomach muscles are how I express my anxiety. One of the early steps of understanding the "ME" system is learning how I experience different emotions.

When I was working in a veteran's hospital, I worked with anger management patients. These were men who had a history of sudden, explosive anger, which they sometimes acted out violently. They sound like frightening people, yet many of them felt helpless. One of my clients, Michael, had very little awareness of when or why he would lash out at others. He felt helpless to change his behavior because he didn't understand why it happened or how to stop it. In his experience, one moment, he was just having a normal argument with his wife, and the next, he would blow up and lash out.

The first part of our work was to help Michael catch the signals of his increasing anger by paying attention to his body. His body could tell him he was getting angry long before his awareness caught on. He could learn to hear his emotions by listening to his body, and as a result, he could slowly learn to experience them rather than act them out. Michael's jaw was his first ally. When he started to get angry, he would clench his teeth, and a muscle would start to flex in his jaw. When he started to pay attention, his jaw was like an early warning system, informing him his anger was heating up. Then other signals came online, including flushing or breathing heavily. Understanding these body signals was the start of Michael's developing emotional intelligence.

Our body knows our experience first. Once we can catch the body signal, we have a better chance of derailing a rage reaction. Reactive people often feel overwhelmed by their feelings. Other people, less in touch with their feelings, might feel cut off from them. We must know what we're experiencing before we can work with it because **there's no behavioral choice without first developing awareness**.

RELATIONSHIP WARRIORSHIP EXERCISE: WHAT IS YOUR BODY TELLING YOU?

- What musical instrument are you? Using musical instruments as a metaphor, what types of instruments make up who you are?

- What are some of the physical signals that your body gives you when you are feeling something? Do you get anxiety butterflies? Do your shoulders ache from stress?

Identifying or Labelling Our Emotions

IDENTIFYING EMOTIONS

Sometimes, we know we're having an emotion because our body is clearly telling us. But **what** exactly are we feeling? Emotions are confusing until we know how to label them. Once the body has notified us, our mind/heart begins to sort out **what** we're feeling, usually based on our past experiences. For example, my eyes tear up when I am angry, frustrated, and sad. So, when I cry, which is it? Am I angry, am I frustrated, or sad? Feelings aren't just black or white, and it takes time to sort them out. Think of a place in your life where you're ambivalent. It's likely that you're having more than one feeling about the situation. There may be multiple emotions stacking up one behind the other, like dominoes. If we struggle with certain emotions, we may also mask them. I think of this as wrapping a romantic novel in a military cover. Maybe I hate feeling vulnerable, so I mask it with a tough exterior.

Interpreting My Emotions

Once we can identify our emotions, we need to make sense of them. Okay, my tense stomach muscles are telling me I'm frustrated. What is going on to make me feel frustrated? What are the thoughts I am having about the situation? These thoughts make up a story about what our body is feeling. "I'm frustrated because it's the third time I have talked to Noriko about this!" Our mental narratives make meaning about what is happening. Everybody's stories are different, and the themes give us a ton of information about ourselves. Do we tend to feel slighted or disrespected? Do the narratives in our minds tell us we are unloved, incompetent, unimportant, or marginalized? Whether these stories are "true" or "untrue" is less important than the fact that they shape our worldview. If your emotions are your instrument, what are some of the pieces of music, the familiar themes, that you routinely play with them?

 ## THE STORIES WE MAKE UP

Back in 2008, Marita and I decided to get married, and we invited our next-door neighbors, whom we didn't know that well. The deadline came for RSVPs, and we still hadn't heard anything from them. As time passed, we began to get annoyed. Why were they ignoring us? This was quickly

followed by the development of a painful narrative. "They aren't saying anything to us about the wedding. It must be because they're homophobic. Here we thought they were friendly people, and now we are finding out that they cannot support two women getting legally married." Following this narrative, we worked ourselves into quite a lather of hurt and indignation. And eventually, we stopped interacting with them.

A week before the wedding, our neighbors rang our doorbell. "Oh, we are so excited! We didn't think we could make your wedding because we had vacation plans for the same date. We didn't want to say anything until we were sure we could change our plans. We've managed to shift our vacation plans, and now, if it's not too late, we'd love to come to your wedding."

Needless to say, we were relieved and ashamed. In the absence of hearing from them, we had made up a whole huge story. While our caring neighbors were working hard to shift their vacation plans, we made up that they were unfriendly and homophobic.

Our minds are full of narratives like this, and we come by them honestly. The world has plenty of homophobic people; we wouldn't have that narrative if we hadn't experienced it before. After a number of painful experiences, we jump to conclusions that can end up closing down the connection. Perhaps we say good morning to a colleague, and they don't answer us. Our face frowns just a bit, and the meaning-making machines in our head start to make up stories, "She must not like me. Is she snubbing me? Did I piss her off?" Another part of developing EQ is to become aware of the meaning-making machinery and to check out your perceptions. If you actually check with your colleague, she may say something like, "Oh, sorry! I was thinking about something and was so preoccupied that I didn't even hear you." A lot of our experience of the world is based on our history. These narratives derive from our cultural upbringing, our personal experiences, and our beliefs.

I want to emphasize that just because I have a "favorite hits" list about myself, and the world does not mean those stories are not at least partially true. Systemic racism, homophobia, and gender bias have been baked into our global society for thousands of years. They are very real and daily experiences for members of these communities. Our narratives are born from painful experiences and history. The single most toxic thing we can do is to deny the reality of systemic oppression by blaming the victim! Our life experience as a woman, a person of color, a disabled person, etc., outfits us with a set of lenses that show us that discrimination is part of our societal architecture. That protective filter helps us to survive in a sometimes-hostile environment. At the same time, part of our evolution is to remain open to checking that filter, checking the narrative to make sure we are not trapped in a belief that is not serving us now. In the above story, Marita and my sensitivity to homophobia was based on experiences of painful hostile bias. We were married less than a week before Proposition 8 blocked the ability for gays and lesbians to marry in California in November 2008. Our discrimination lens was accurate about the social climate at that time. However, it was NOT accurate about suspecting homophobia in our neighbors. To evolve as people, we need to become aware of how we make meaning about our experiences and then double-check to make sure those narratives still apply.

Everybody is right partially."

– CRR GLOBAL

There is a difference between objective fact and subjective experience. In the above story, our feelings of hurt and anger were valid experiences, even if the facts were incorrect. What someone feels is a very real experience and cannot be denied. Your feelings are always valid because they are your experience! My internal experience is what it is. However, my neighbors were not snubbing our wedding because they were homophobic, and those feelings may not be based on objective facts.

It is important to distinguish between objective, measurable facts and subjective feelings, especially since we are apt to conflate the two. In 2017, a poll by Public Policy Polling found that 1 percent of Americans believed the Earth was flat, with an additional 6 percent saying they weren't sure.

For every individual, my felt experience is subjectively "true" for me, regardless of the objective facts of things. The power of my subjective narrative will frequently override objective fact. In May 2021 in the United States, it was estimated by a Reuters/Ipsos opinion poll that as many as 53 percent of Republicans still believed the election was stolen from Donald Trump.[22]

Many counts, recounts, certifications, and dozens of court cases have demonstrated that this is **not** factually true. Biden factually, numerically, objectively won the election. Regardless of how many times these objective facts are presented to Trump supporters, their subjective narrative, their emotions, tell them that the election was stolen. Not only do their feelings inform them, but they are also listening to a completely different set of facts. Democrats and Republicans are not looking through the same lens in terms of objective news, and their narratives are divergent. If we refuse to acknowledge the truth of how Trump supporters are feeling, we run the risk of disconnecting with large parts of the country.

To evolve in relationship, we need to constantly examine our stories about the world. Are they true? Partially true?[23] Or did we just make

---

22 According to a May 2021 Reuters/Ipsos opinion poll, "*The Big Lie: Over half of Republicans believe Donald Trump is the actual President of the United States,*" 53 percent of Republicans believed that Trump was the "true president," compared with 3 percent of Democrats and 25 percent of all Americans, over a year after the election results.

23 We couldn't write this section without referencing Byron Katie's "The Work." The Work is a simple but powerful practice that allows people to not only remain alert to their stressful thoughts—the ones that cause all the anger, sadness, and frustration in our world—but also question them, and through that questioning the thoughts lose their power. To use Katie's words: "Great spiritual texts describe the what—what it means to be free. The Work is the how. It shows you exactly how to identify and question any thought that would keep you from that freedom."

the whole thing up? How do I even know what is true? My **experience** always feels true for me, and it is totally valid as my **experience**. And in a relationship, how I am feeling may trump objective truth.

It is important to know that our narratives lead to action. As a result of Marita's and my narrative, we didn't talk to our neighbors for several weeks. A key component of EQ is being willing to question our story. What is the impact of being prone to certain narratives, whether they are true or not? One of the ground rules we hold is that "Everybody is right partially." Someone's **experience** is always valid. Their story about the experience may not be factually correct, but it is emotionally valid for them. Ignore it at your peril. Yet, what is the impact of that narrative on our relationships and on our country? Eckhardt Tolle, a spiritual teacher and author of *The Power of Now*, said that: "If you identify with a mental position, then if you are wrong, your mind-based sense of self is seriously threatened with annihilation. So you, as the ego, cannot afford to be wrong. To be wrong is to die. Wars have been fought over this, and countless relationships have broken down." His implication is that war is the inability to tolerate an alternative narrative.

Narratives are not always a problem. They are a normal function of being a human being. Since we are meaning-making machines, narratives are how we interpret and creatively interact with the world. They are also the currency of relationship. Narratives bind the emotions of our lives together and help us to make sense of the world. We are constantly making up a story of who we are in this moment, together or alone. Our love affair is a story we weave between us about how we met, the obstacles we overcame, and the narrative of the Third Entity. Narratives give us maps of the world and create significance. As long as we remind ourselves that it is a **narrative, not a fact,** we can see stories as a source of richness in our lives.

RELATIONSHIP WARRIORSHIP EXERCISE: NARRATIVES

Think about a conflict you had recently.

- What narratives/stories did you make up about what happened?

- What was the impact of holding that story on your situation?

- Did you get the chance to check out your narrative with the other people?

- What part of your narrative was shared by your partner? What part was different?

Expressing Emotions

EXPRESSING EMOTIONS

So, we have identified our feelings and become aware of our narratives, and now it is time to communicate.

Expressing our emotions skillfully is a lifetime journey. As parents, we spend time helping our kids to develop their EQ around communicating, "Johnny, please use your words," "It sounds like you are angry?" "If you could have told Sally what you wanted instead of hitting her, what would you have said?"

Emotions are an energy pressure building up around a need to express. There are so many ways we can choose to communicate! The most primitive form of expression is acting out the feelings physically rather than identifying and saying them out loud. Instead of grieving something, we might get drunk. Or we might lose our temper and throw something. Sometimes we just stuff our feelings down. When we are acting out our feelings, there is less reflection time between the feeling and the physical manifestation of them.

It is also hard to explain how we feel if our affective language is limited in a certain emotional area. For example, it may be easy for us to articulate anger, but we freeze when expressing vulnerability. Cultures vary in which emotions are acceptable to express and the socially appropriate ways to express them. Western cultures often rely on words, but some cultures might express themselves in dance or song.[24]

Our comfort with expressing our feelings is based, in part, on the messages we received as we grew up. We are all more comfortable with certain feelings over others. To continue the "self as musical instrument" analogy, some instruments are better at evoking certain feelings than others. If you lean towards being a drum, it may be more challenging to express tenderness. Harps may have trouble communicating rage. Becoming a coach, a therapist, or a parent, is a powerful way to find out

---

24 Our language also leads to different forms of expression. We would recommend watching Lera Boroditsky's TED talk, "How language shapes the way we think." According to Boroditsky, "The beauty of linguistic diversity is that it reveals to us just how ingenious and how flexible the human mind is. Human minds have invented not one cognitive universe, but 7,000."

which emotions we are uncomfortable with. When you are working with couples or your own family, which emotions make you squirm? Many of us sweat during a conflict, but others get embarrassed by moments of affection. Which emotions are the squirmy ones for **you** to express in your own relationships? Which are the feelings you would prefer to avoid communicating about?

Deploying Emotions

DEPLOYING EMOTIONS

The final step in developing our emotional intelligence is the ability to leverage our emotions to produce a particular outcome. We don't just communicate the energy of emotions; we can also use them consciously, for a purpose. We often see this in strong leaders. Martin Luther King or John Lewis could take the pain of racism and hold it long enough to craft an extraordinary speech or create a march. Emotions are energy; they can be used to power events.

Another powerful example comes from Cantor Fitzgerald, a trading company occupying the 101st to 105th floors of the north tower at the World Trade Center. The company lost 658 of 960 New York-based employees during the attacks on 9/11. Yet the survivors were able to harness their grief over their colleagues and use that pain as fuel to bring the company together. With a skeleton crew, they were able to provide services to their clients and develop action plans to help the families of the dead.

CEO Howard Lutnick was late arriving at the office that day after taking his son to his first day of kindergarten. Among the dead were his brother, Gary, and his best friend, Doug. In an interview for NBC NY News, Lutnick said: "My goal after 9/11 was to take care of the families of the people we lost, and that was the most important thing." And in a matter of days, they pulled together and created purpose out of the pain. For five years, they set aside 25 percent of their profits for the families of those who died, which in the end amounted to $180 million. Despite the catastrophic loss, Cantor was able to use their pain to benefit others.

Emotions can be used for good and for ill. It is how we deploy those emotions that make the difference. Cantor Fitzgerald was able to channel their emotions into something deeply important. It's also possible to use feelings of paranoia and fear as a galvanizing political weapon to radicalize a nation.

Emotions are the language of relationship. We engender emotions in one another, exchange them, amplify them, or avoid them. A relationship with no emotions has no life. This is true for both intimate and work relationships. Even at work (often encouraged to be a feelings-free space), emotions are king. We are inspired by a creative project, bored with administrative work, irritated by a colleague, and burned out by conflicts. We spend thousands of dollars on measuring company morale or team climate. The emotional life of a team is a prime indicator of its health.

The capacity to deploy these emotions for the support of many is also dependent on the next intelligence: social intelligence.

SOCIAL INTELLIGENCE (SI)

"It is Social Intelligence, rather than quantitative intelligence, that defines who we are as humans."

– NICHOLAS HUMPHREY, NEUROPSYCHOLOGIST

Social Intelligence (SI)

Sometimes referred to as emotional/social intelligence (ESI), we are now shifting over to the YOU/ME system. Having learned to play my own emotional instrument, I now want to have a duet with someone else. It's easy to see that the more competent I am with my own emotions, the easier it will be to make music with someone else.

"**Social intelligence** is the expansion of EQ into a capacity to understand and empathize with someone else. Not only can I feel, understand and appropriately express my own emotions, but I can also feel, understand and empathize with another person's experience. I can hear their emotional music. I can accurately read another person with minimal projection or displacement of my own feelings."

– CRR GLOBAL

Social intelligence (SI) recognizes that we are social beings. With emotional intelligence, I begin to understand the complexity of my own system. With social intelligence, I begin to understand the complexity of the people around me. Sometimes social intelligence refers to the collective, but for the sake of this book, we are going to define it as my relationship with one other person or the YOU/ME system.

With the YOU/ME connection, my world is expanded, and a dance begins between the complexity of who they are and the complexity of who I am. I referred to this dance earlier when I spoke about how I love most of Marita's aspects, tolerate others, and actively dislike a few.

Let's shift our analogy to dancing with another person. In every interaction, a part of Faith is dancing with a part of Marita, and some dances are more successful than others. Marita and I do very well when we are speaking publicly about systemic coaching. Our "public speaker" selves are highly collaborative, and we flow together well. But our "course design selves" are both very opinionated and a bit territorial. They tend to wrestle for control. So, designing can be stressful for our relationship, but public speaking is fun. Within each of us is a multitude of subpersonalities that lead to a geometric set of interactions together. No wonder partnerships are so rich, varied, and complex! Each unique partnership has the potential to stimulate, inspire, irritate, and provoke us. This is true for both professional and personal relationships.

The deep YOU/ME systems in our lives, like a spouse, child, or long-term business partner, are the transformative forces of our lives. They get under our skin, mold us, demand from us, and call us forth. They are the people who inspire us on our journey of Relationship Warriorship. Relationship Warriorship is critical because **transformative relationships are not just about being happy.** Somewhere along the way, Western culture got hooked on the romantic belief of finding the perfect soul mate or business partner and living happily ever after. While I am as addicted to the romantic moment as the rest of us, this is a profoundly impoverished view of relationships. Yes, we all long for and need those blissfully intimate or creative moments! But a lifetime of nothing but blissful moments would be like eating your favorite dessert as the main course for every single meal.

Wait a minute, I hear a voice cry, *I would **love** to eat my favorite dessert for every meal!* I get it, isn't the goal of life to be happy? Certainly, we all need and want happiness in our lives. But there are huge areas of positivity research that are trying to figure out what happiness even means. Spiritual leaders suggest that happiness is an inside job, the result of finding meaning and compassion. Positive psychology includes feelings of gratitude and flow. Certainly, joy and happiness are critical components of YOU/ME relationships. However, this book is about the path of Right Relationship as a way to grow and evolve as a person. And growth is rarely easy. There is actually such a thing as toxic positivity. The transformative relationships of our lives are the ones that impact us profoundly, for better or worse. Some of the people who grow us include beloved partners who teach us that we are worthy of love. But many relationships are harsher teachers. The devastating loss, the severe critic, the malicious enemy, and the life-threatening illness are also partners that confront us with difficult truths. Our responses to those difficult events carve out our character just as profoundly as happy ones do. It may be a design flaw in the universe, but the times of ease and bliss often allow us to coast. The painful challenges force us to rise to the occasion.

The Harvard Study of Adult Development (often referred to as the Grant Study after its founder, W. T. Grant) was a seminal project that has tracked its subjects for almost eighty years. One of the instruments they used to track their subjects was a yearly questionnaire about different aspects of their lives. In the section evaluating the subjects' marriages was the question, "Have you ever considered divorce?" One year, the researchers received a questionnaire where the word divorce was heavily crossed out. In the margin was written, "Murder, yes, divorce, no."

For me, this simple anecdote sums up the double-edged power of even a good marriage. Our partners **will** shape us. They are our collaborators in co-evolution. Often it is the hard moments in marriage that force us to grow into Right Relationship.

On a day-to-day basis, our parents, bosses, spouses, teams, siblings, and kids tumble us like stones in a rock tumbler, grinding off our edges and smoothing our character.

Other difficult life experiences may be more devasting. There are relationship traumas that take years to recover from, or that we never recover from. An interesting question is, **"What do we mean by 'recover'?"** If we hope to go back to normal, to the way we were, we will likely be disappointed.

The more traumatic the event, the more we will be changed. These events will shape us for better or worse, like a tree that crashes down on top of another tree, warping its growth pattern.[25]

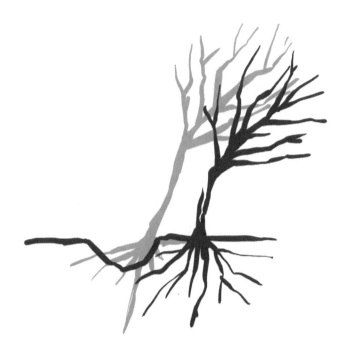

Things will never go back to the way they were. The best we can do is take the time to absorb the shock and begin to create meaning from it. A profound loss, like a death or a betrayal, may take years to shape us and have different narrative stages. We may need to go through all Kübler-Ross' stages of shock, denial, bargaining, anger, and grief.[26] We may never reach acceptance, and what does acceptance even mean? We never really

25 In her powerful 2018 TED Talk, "We don't move on from grief. We move forward with it," Nora McInery shares her hard-earned wisdom about life and death. Most powerfully, she encourages us to shift how we approach grief. "A grieving person is going to laugh again and smile again," she says. "They're going to move forward. But that doesn't mean that they've moved on."

26 Elizabeth Kübler-Ross is a Swiss-American psychiatrist and pioneer in near-death studies. In her 1969 book *On Death and Dying*, Kübler-Ross proposed the patient-focused, death-adjustment pattern, the "Five Stages of Grief." The five stages are denial, anger, bargaining, depression, and acceptance.

accept the death of a beloved person. Their presence/absence will always be part of our life. The relationship will always be there, but its shape has changed. How do we include the devastating loss and let it leave its mark, its truth, and still integrate the experience we gain from it?

Sometimes, the best we can do is to use the loss, the bankruptcy, or the divorce, to create a narrative that might support life in some way, like Cantor Fitzgerald did. The transformation of a relationship trauma into possibilities is slow and painful.

It brings to mind the Japanese ceramic practice of honoring a broken pottery piece through the practice of Kintsugi. Pottery is beautiful and fragile. When you hold a cup, you know that sooner or later, this cup will get broken. The ephemeral nature of pottery is part of its beauty. We appreciate it even more, knowing it is not forever. And when a piece does break, a kintsugi potter takes the pieces of the cup and solders the broken pieces together with gold.

KINTSUGI

YOU/ME relationships are fragile and easily broken by circumstance. Can we honor whom we love knowing they must and will change? Are we able to take a betrayal, a disappointment, and repair the pieces with gold? And if not, can we honor the permanence of the break and let it be our teacher for the future? So much Relationship Warriorship is needed to get through these harrowing events.

Perhaps you are thinking, *"This all sounds great, but **how** do I create kintsugi with a broken relationship?"* There is no glib answer, no map for this. Dealing with the blows of our life will be different for every single person. And some of us don't recover from it.

There are a few things that can help but no easy solutions.

RELATIONSHIP WARRIORSHIP WITH LOSS

Acknowledge that you are in relationship with the loss. It happened, it is happening, and your experience is real. Big losses are like a spotlight shining in your face from four inches away. All you can see is that spotlight, and you cannot turn away. Over time, that painful spotlight will slowly move away, inch by inch, and there will be more things to see around it. But although it may recede deeply over the years, it may never go away. That loss is part of your life.

Be gentle with yourself and others. There are many phases and stages with loss, and every phase has its own timeline. Grief, rage, isolation, suicidality, blaming, guilt, denial, and self-medicating may all show up. Each part of grief requires so much Relationship Warriorship. Loss is an emotional storm, and there is no state of mind abnormal to it. Let those emotions visit; let them storm through. Just do your best not to invite the storms to live in your house permanently. Losses like a death or severe illness can have deep collateral damage on a family. Remember you are in relationship with others who are struggling too. What does Right Relationship mean together, moment to moment?

Get the help you need to keep walking the journey together with others who are affected. Coaching, therapy, support groups, etc., can give you a place to process the loss without having to act it out destructively with others.

When the grief spotlight has moved back a bit, stand in Lion's Roar as much as you can (see page 24 for a recap of this). Loss will permanently shape you. **How** it shapes you will, in part, be up to you. Ultimately, you will have some choice about what lessons/stories you will draw from it. You may need to make some decisions. Will I turn onto a permanent path of bitterness or cynicism? Will I close my heart to avoid any future pain? How will my narrative impact my future choices?

Forgive yourself and others. Loss is a hard taskmaster. You will fail, fall down, and hurt others and yourself sometimes. Especially forgive yourself. We cannot always practice Relationship Warriorship. Sometimes, we just can't make lemonade with the lemons life gives us.

The power of a relationship is not its longevity; it is its impact and the meaning we make out of it. What did we learn from it? Can we use that painful event to grow, or will we contract and shrink?

RELATIONSHIP SYSTEMS INTELLIGENCE (RSI) – WORKING WITH THE *WE* OF LARGER SYSTEMS

The third intelligence building block is Relationship Systems Intelligence (RSI). This intelligence can be applied to any kind of system, the ME, the YOU/ME, and WE collectives spanning from teams to families, to whole organizations. Relationship Systems Intelligence is CRR Global's contribution to the intelligence conversation. It includes and transcends the concepts of emotional intelligence and social intelligence and offers what we believe is the next evolution in the intelligence field: Relationship Systems Intelligence (RSI).

We have touched on the complexity of the multiple MEs that I have inside and the complexity of the system of YOU/ME where all my selves inter-act with all of your selves. Now, we are moving into the Third Entity of a system of many people, or the WE. Naturally, WE systems have a Third Entity just like the YOU/ME systems do. They are as complex and alive as smaller relationship systems, and Relationship Systems Intelligence is our ability to connect with these larger collectives.

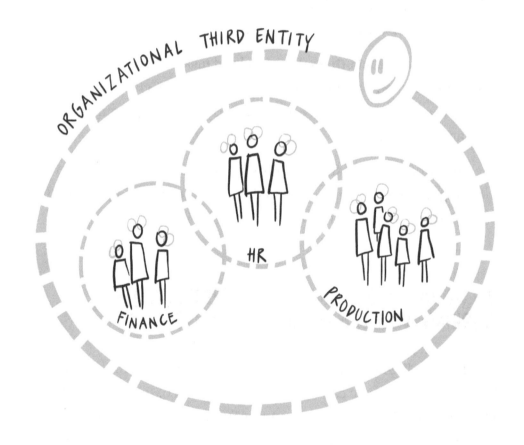

"**Relationship Systems Intelligence** is the ability to experience a team, organization, family, or community as a fluid, interacting, energetic system or Third Entity. Within that relationship system, each individual and nested system is a voice of that system."

— CRR GLOBAL

When we shift to the WE, an internal shift is required. We are now working with larger groups of people or with systemic entities like departments. Instead of seeing a group of individuals, we shift our perception to seeing one system, a Third Entity, with its own character, strengths, and needs. Within the WE system, there are usually nested systems. For example, within every organization are nested individuals (ME), pairs (YOU/ME), and departments like HR, management, or sales (WE).

Emotional intelligence helped me to play my own instrument. Social intelligence taught me to play a duet with another. Now, we are playing with a whole symphony of instruments. Will our teams or families create a cacophony, or will we sound like Mozart? Here is where the concept of the Third Entity is particularly important. We can view a WE system as a collection of competing instruments, *or* we can view it as one entity, the orchestra. When we are working with a larger system (whether that is a family or an organization), our job is to help that orchestra to find its song. How do we bring together all these disparate instruments into one expression of the whole? We cannot listen to the oboes or violins alone. We are listening to the sound of the whole organization's music. We may adjust one department or individual to bring up the volume of management or cue in the CEO, but it is in service of the sound of the whole company orchestra. Each instrument or section of that organizational orchestra is a vital part and needs to be heard. When we are standing in Relationship Systems Intelligence, we are always listening for the overall song of the system. Each member of that system makes a unique and critical contribution to its overall functioning, but that contribution is one expression of the whole.

We can think of the three intelligences, ME, YOU/ME, and WE, as the three legs of the relationship systems stool. And all three legs of the stool are needed to have a stable system.

Pulling the Three Legs of the Stool Together

THREE LEGGED STOOL

ME WE

ME/YOU

To be good at relationships, we need to be able to shift our perspective from one kind of intelligence to another. For example, think of the Third Entity exercise you did in the YOU/ME section above. When you stood in the ME corner of the triangle, you were working on emotional intelligence. You were articulating what **you** felt and what **you** wanted around your disturbance with another person. In the YOU corner, you were working on social intelligence. You were doing your best to feel into what your partner might feel or want. When you stood in the third position, you gave voice to the relationship's Third Entity, placing you firmly into Relationship Systems Intelligence. Speaking from each of these perspectives helps us to understand the situation from a different leg of the intelligence stool. Our understanding has expanded from the personal to a much larger perspective on the issue.

The relationship stool will lose its stability if one of its legs is wobbly. It will be unbalanced if one leg is longer than any other. We need to nurture all three legs: our relationship with our self, our relationship with others, and our relationships with the Third Entity. Organizational and Relationship Systems Coaching (ORSC) considers all these pieces and recognizes that any system is only as great as the sum of its parts. Systems thinking offers us a wider lens and a helicopter view of the relationship systems we are a part of.

Let's apply the three legs of the intelligence stool using the below example.

Sally is a manager of a research team. Her team complains that she is uncollaborative and tends to micromanage. Let's look at her situation through the lens of three intelligences.

- *Sally's ME: Sally is a scientist just promoted to a management position, and she was given no management training. With no experience or training, she naturally lacks an understanding of how to behave as a manager. Her emotional intelligence needs some support in this area.*

- *YOU/ME: Sally wants her team to respect her, so she over-functions. Trying to be helpful, she hovers over each researcher's project, which makes them feel overmanaged. She wants to contribute but tends to take over their research. This stool leg is social intelligence.*

- *WE: Morale drops, and the team members complain that Sally does not trust them to do their work independently. They make their discomfort known on the organizational climate survey (Relationship Systems Intelligence).*

So, how might we support Sally in this situation? Well, we could probably start with any leg of the intelligence stool.

Let's start with the Relationship Systems Intelligence perspective revealed by the information from the organizational climate survey.

- *When Sally gets poor reviews on the organizational climate survey, her supervisor can get curious. "Sally, what is going on for you, that has your direct reports saying that you are overmanaging them?" This question taps into Sally's EQ.*

- *The SI leg of the stool helps Sally to confide in her supervisor that she feels she needs more training in management skills. "I'm a researcher, and I'm just not trained in how to manage my direct reports (EQ). Can I get some management training (SI and RSI)?"*

- *Hopefully, Sally will get more management training and feels more confident about supporting her team (improved EQ, SI, and RSI levels).*

- *She can communicate better with each team member and micro-manages less (SI).*

- *Team morale improves on the following survey (RSI).*

In this oversimplified example, we can see how all three legs of the stool are needed and how each affects the other. This is equally true for family systems. Each leg of the intelligence stool provides a different understanding of any situation.

Pedro and Anna are separating after sixteen years of marriage. They have three children, Thomas (fifteen), Manuel (thirteen), and Lucia (nine). Understandably, this is a difficult time for the whole family (RSI). Thomas blames his father for the separation and is very angry with him (EQ, SI). Manuel spends time out of the house talking with his friends about the divorce (SI, RSI). Lucia complains she has a stomach ache and doesn't want to go to school (EQ). When Manual is arrested for shoplifting, the whole thing comes to a head with the family (RSI). The family goes into coaching together and explores how each person is struggling (EQ, SI, RSI). Each child reacts to the separation in their own unique way, and the family works on sharing feelings more and acting them out less (EQ, SI, RSI). Thomas and his father have facilitated conversations about working through their anger (SI). The parents work with the legal system to get Manuel put on probation (RSI). Lucia gets some individual support to help her express her anxiety verbally rather than expressing it through her stomach (EQ).

These examples vividly show the interplay between the three kinds of intelligence. It also shows the expanding nature of systemic disturbances. If a problem on any leg of the stool is not addressed, it will expand to all three legs. Personal issues will affect the family or the business. Organizational issues create personal burnout and relationship problems. In the case of the family above, the disturbance of the YOU/ME system of Pedro and Anna impacts everyone individually (ME) and the family system as a whole (WE). Finally, unresolved systemic issues may radiate out to affect larger community systems such as the police, the courts, family therapy, etc. This is the nature of systems; they are interconnected and interactive, each systemic holon affecting the next.

The exercise below will give you a feel for the different levels of systems and how they build upon one another. We use this exercise in our fundamentals course to help people get an experiential feel for being in nested systems. Use your imagination, and we hope you will be able to get a sense of the different levels of systems. Give it a try and keep it playful!

RELATIONSHIP WARRIORSHIP EXERCISE: THE STRING EXERCISE

The Scenario: Joining a New Organization

Imagine you are interviewing for a position with the management team at International Climate Advocates (ICA). There are five people in the management team: the CEO, the Operations Manager, the Finance Manager, the Marketing Manager, and the International Partners Manager. You are joining them for a job interview for the position of IT Manager for the company. To navigate the hiring process, you will need to connect with all three systemic levels (ME, YOU/ME, and WE) and access all three kinds of intelligence.

The ME System

Of course, the first level of intelligence is the "ME" system (EQ). Imagine that you are holding a piece of string in your two hands. Even better, go get a string to play with. **To get a feel for this exercise, try putting up your hands as if holding an imaginary string.**

The string represents the relationship between different parts of the ME system, which have different feelings about joining the ICA. The hand on the left in the above graphic is the part inside of you that

is excited to join the ICA. That part of you that says YES because you believe in the ICA mission and love the idea of working for an international company. But your other hand is the part of you that has doubts about joining the company (NO). The ICA is a start-up, and you know many start-ups fail. The NO hand really wants a more stable, secure job right now. So emotionally, you are split. The YES hand is pulling the string towards joining the ICA, saying, "I would love to work for this company," and the NO hand is pulling away from the ICA, "No, I need a secure job right now." As these two interior voices pull you in different directions, tension arises in the string. **You** are the whole string, with all those different voices pulling and tugging inside of you about what decisions to make.

Anytime you have mixed feelings about something, your internal conflicts about the topic will make you feel tense. For example, if the "fight" between your YES hand and your NO hand is too intense, it can actually snap the string. That might manifest in not taking the job. Or that snap may manifest itself in literally "snapping" at someone, or it could even show up as a physical symptom like a migraine.

So, this is your ME relationship system: many different voices inside you pulling on you to go in different directions. Noticing and understanding these different parts of yourself is the realm of emotional intelligence. This is the experience of the first leg of the stool.

Everyone within the ICA management team is having a ME conversation within themselves, all invisibly, of course, but it's happening as each person internally debates and thinks about hiring a new IT person. Each person is having a silent conversation inside themselves, "Should we hire this person or not? Do we really need this position now? How will we pay for it?"

The YOU/ME (SI) System

FINANCIAL MANAGER   INTERVIEWEE

The next phase of the hiring process consists of you having individual interviews with different members of the management team. So, now we are moving into the YOU/ME, social intelligence system. In a YOU/ME system, one person holds one end of the invisible relationship string, and the other person holds the other end. The string is the relationship between the two of you as you talk together. This relationship string will tighten or loosen from moment to moment, depending on the emotional field between the two of you. If there is not enough connection between the two of you, the relationship string may feel slack. Other times, it may get tense or even tie itself in a knot, depending on how the conversation is going.

You may find that one of your ME selves is jockeying for better compensation. That self may pull on the string (raise the tension) between yourself and the financial manager. The financial manager must decide whether to pull back and resist the raise or go along with your proposal and let you pull her along into a higher salary. If the financial manager offers less compensation than you need, the relationship string between you could snap, and you would walk away from the job. The conversation is complex because, as we mentioned before, all your ME selves are interacting with all of the ME selves of the financial manager. So, there's a lot going on in the YOU/ME string connection. Face to face, you are just having a conversation, but there are many other dynamics going on beneath the surface. You're having an SI conversation invisibly through the string. The words you speak together and the energetic interaction between the two of you will determine what happens in the relationship. **All of this is going on all the time** in any conversation. Usually, we are just not aware of it.

Of course, this YOU/ME conversation is going on throughout the ICA management system. Pairs are forming and having conversations that are shaping each other's decisions. This YOU/ME conversation through the string is social intelligence, the second leg of the stool.

The WE System (Larger Relationship Collective)

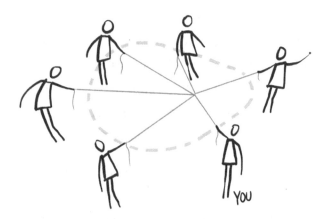

Now imagine that the YOU/ME interviews are complete, and the management team has decided to hire you. The management team gets together with you to onboard and orient you to their system. The Third Entity of the management team (WE) now includes you. Of course, everyone in the system is still resonating with relationship strings on the ME and YOU/ME levels. At the same time, all

six of you are communicating on the WE level of the management team. All of yourselves and all of their selves are interconnected. This is the larger WE system, the Third Entity of the management team.

In the graphic above, you can see that the management team relationship web holds and is responsible for all the content of ICA company. The employees, the projects, the budgets, all the endeavors of the company are held within the net of those relationships. The management team is a Third Entity of interconnected people, supporting the company together.

We can feel this web in our interactions together. It's like a spider web; if you pull on one thread, the whole web moves in response. The management team Third Entity is constantly moving and shifting and interacting with different aspects of the web. This, in turn, pulls on the rest of the web, creating directional pressures, tensions, looseness, etc. We can often feel these changes through the relational web, though we rarely talk about them.

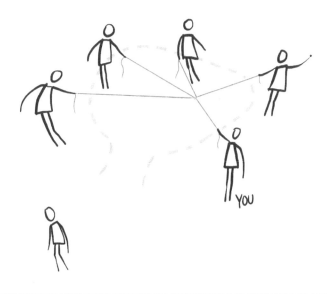

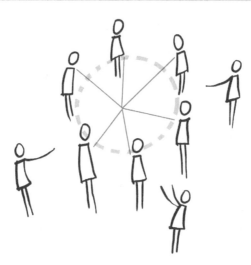

Let's imagine that the marketing manager decides that she is going to leave the ICA. All the strings that she holds are suddenly dropped. So, there are now gaps in the web. Nobody in the system interacts with her clients or handles her sales targets. The entire Management team must compensate for those holes that have opened up by stepping in and holding critical tasks until someone new is hired. So, the remaining senior managers are stressed as they scramble to cover up the gaps in the web.

Eventually, the ICA is ready to hire someone to replace the marketing manager, but this time, they hire two people, one for marketing and one for sales. Now, the management team will have to adjust again to allow the new sales and new marketing manager to weave into the management team's Third Entity web.

Individual Impact on the Web

The graphic of the management team web helps us to clearly see how interconnected every team is. It is impossible for anything to happen without it impacting the whole.

Let's imagine the financial manager fights with you about something, and you become frustrated. Your irritability will leak into the management team and will start to put stress on the whole web. Your mood is pulling on the emotional field of the web, creating tension and tightness. It is beginning to affect the entire system, even though you might not be aware of your impact.

Relationship Systems Intelligence is the ability to sense the whole relationship web of the system—the ability to see the invisible frame of interacting strings holding us all together. So, when we come from the Relationship Systems Intelligence perspective, we know that every individual is a critical point on that web and is having an impact. **Relationship Systems Intelligence focuses on the relationship strings within the WE.** The practice of Relationship Systems Intelligence is to focus on the web, not just the people.

Working with a large system can feel very overwhelming. All those different people, all those nested systems, different dynamics, and all that complexity is a lot to encompass. Things get easier when we develop the ability to change our focal length view. Do we need to be able to see the twenty separate individuals within the department? Yes. But we also need to be able to see the forest instead of the trees. Can we look at the string as well as the people? We want to be able to zoom out from the twenty individuals and look at their interaction as a system. What is the status of this department as a systemic Third Entity? Is it healthy? Stressed? Growing? Conflicted? What is the pain of this system, and how is that pain signaling a need to grow or change?

Just like individuals, teams and families are entities with problems, strengths, and purpose. In a family, we need to be able to focus on the individual needs of an autistic child, yet we also must perceive the impact of that focus on the rest of the family.

When we can come from Relationship Systems Intelligence, life becomes bigger but also simpler. Once we start to see relationship systems, we see them everywhere. Suddenly, we're surrounded by relationship systems that are connected to one another. We become increasingly aware of how the energetic connections between people are affecting the whole team or family. **Suddenly, it becomes less about who is doing what to whom and more about what is trying to happen for the whole system.** The ability to move our perspective fluidly between intelligences is a critical relationship and leadership skill. Can I track and articulate my own experience? Do I accurately know what is going on for my colleague or my child? What is going on in the larger company or family system?

This concludes the basics section of this book. Hopefully, it gives you some key concepts we need to grow in relationship. To sum it up:

- If we are going to survive as a species, we need to evolve our ability to get on better with one another. We need to strive for Right Relationship.

- The Third Entity helps us to get there. It gives us the ability to see, hear, and sense the systems around us. Right Relationship Warriorship gives us the courage and awareness to walk that path.

- The three intelligences, EQ, SI, and RSI, provide the awareness to detect and work with the three levels of relationship systems: the ME, YOU/ME, and the WE.

- Once we have learned to see, hear, and sense systems, our perception of relationships changes. It's like getting a new car, and now you see that car everywhere. Suddenly, you are encountering relationship systems all around you.

- You also have some RSI tools to help you work with those systems: the Paper Constellation (ME), the Third Entity (YOU/ME), and the String Exercise (WE).

Now that we can detect these systemic entities, in the next section, we will learn about their habits. What are the attributes of relationships? What can we expect? How do they behave?

PART 2

THE PRINCIPLES OF RELATIONSHIP SYSTEMS INTELLIGENCE (RSI)

CHAPTER 11

INTRODUCTION TO THE PRINCIPLES – HOW RELATIONSHIP SYSTEMS BEHAVE

"A principle is a proposition or value that is a guide for behavior or evaluation."

— CRR GLOBAL

The above gives us a formal definition of a principle. However, we prefer to think of principles as **the bones of something.** Regardless of how something moves, grows, or changes, the bones create the structure that the rest of the body hangs on. So, principles are part of the organizing qualities of something. Like any entity, a relationship system has certain principles or structural bones that help us to understand and predict its behavior. The next few chapters will introduce you to some of these. Regardless of whether it is a ME system, a YOU/ME system, or a WE system, the principles help us to understand how that relationship system works. Understanding the principles is the training ground of the Relationship Warrior.

For example, if we're studying lions, first, we must learn about them. How do they look, smell, sound, and behave? Each individual lion is unique, but each is also part of the Third Entity of the collective lion species. All lions have some common qualities. It is useful to know how they function so we can predict their behavior when we face some on the trail! In the same way, this book will give you some organizing principles that will build your RSI and help you predict the behavior of relationships.

Relationship Systems have dozens of attributes, but we will be focusing on five of the major ones. As you interact with your family, community, or company, these are some things you can expect. Each principle gives a different insight into what might be happening in the relationship and why. The principles will also help you to predict what might be happening next. To be forewarned is to be forearmed. This section of the book will also include more RSI tools and skills, and we will provide you with questions and exercises that will allow you to apply what you're learning to the systems in your life. The principles can be used like a diagnostic tool. Which of these principles is showing up in your own relationship systems?

It's important to remember that these principles are tendencies, not laws. Each system is also unique. Just because the last pride of lions didn't eat you is no guarantee that the next pride won't. Principles may not be operating all the time. They are **not** linear or causal; they are interdependent and interactive. We will describe them in a certain order, but each principle impacts the others.[27]

---

27 For more information about the application of the principles to professional environments, we would recommend looking at the following books: *Creating Intelligent Teams: Leading with Relationship Systems Intelligence* by Anne Rød and Marita Fridjhon and *Systems Inspired Leadership* by Frank Uit de Weerd and Marita Fridjhon.

THE PRINCIPLES OF RELATIONSHIP SYSTEMS

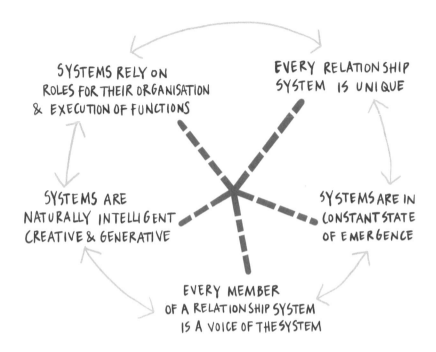

SYSTEMS RELY ON
ROLES FOR THEIR ORGANISATION
& EXECUTION OF FUNCTIONS

EVERY RELATIONSHIP
SYSTEM IS UNIQUE

SYSTEMS ARE
NATURALLY INTELLIGENT
CREATIVE & GENERATIVE

SYSTEMS ARE IN
CONSTANT STATE
OF EMERGENCE

EVERY MEMBER
OF A RELATIONSHIP SYSTEM
IS A VOICE OF THE SYSTEM

CHAPTER 12

PRINCIPLE – EVERY RELATIONSHIP SYSTEM IS UNIQUE

EVERY RELATIONSHIP SYSTEM
IS UNIQUE

Just as every person has their own character and personality, so does every systemic third entity. What is fascinating and daunting about working with relationship systems is that everyone is different. What worked with the last family or team won't necessarily work with the next. One size does not fit all.

Of course, the size of a system contributes to the stability of its attributes. Larger WE systems have a certain mass or weight, which impacts their members. Systems are like boats of different sizes. YOU/ME systems, or pairs, behave like a small sailboat. Pairs move and shift easily and somewhat unpredictably, like a small sailboat in changing winds.[28] Larger systems like teams or organizations are like freighters. Ponderous, they take longer to change direction and need more time to respond to influences. Generally speaking, the larger the system, the longer it takes to change. The ME system may shift in a few minutes. WE systems, like countries, can take generations to move.

Every Third Entity has its own unique character and personality, just like every person does. Before we can interact effectively with a pair or a community group, we must get to know it. This is easy to do when you think of couples and families. We can instinctively feel that each family is unique in its values, warmth, and style of conflict. We may resonate more with one unique family system than with another. We naturally have affinities with some relationships more than others. This is also true of larger systems. Think of some of the teams or community systems you interact with and consider their character. Is the team quiet and low energy? Are they rebellious and challenging? Playful? Confused? Overwhelmed? By considering the *qualities* of the system's culture, we create space to step back and get a meta-view of the Third Entity. Relationship systems are like people. They don't just have behaviors. They also have an emotional life, an atmosphere, and a belief system. And as with individuals, we will get along better with some systems than with others.

---

28 This why couples coaching can keep you on your toes, as the changes can be rapid!

THE METAPHOR GAME

When we assess a system with formal assessments like The Group Leadership Circle Profile or DISC, we're basically conducting a team personality test. What does this system believe? How does it act? What does it feel?

A more subjective way to get the character of a system is to play the metaphor game with them. If the team had to come up with a metaphor or an image for themselves, what would it be? We worked with one high-powered brokerage company that said their team was a Ferrari. They were fast, powerful, and competitive! They felt great about this image until we asked, **"What are some disadvantages to being a high-performance Ferrari?"** After laughing, they said that it broke down too easily, was expensive to maintain, and it was hard to replace parts. This image opened the door to talk about stress and resilience with a proud and high-powered team.

By embracing the uniqueness of each team and using a metaphor, we can go into relationship with it. For example, we worked with one non-profit where the founder was retiring. To her credit, she wanted the company to feel well-prepared and was doing a thorough job of planning for the transition. However, the team was beginning to feel overmanaged, and when we brainstormed a team metaphor, they came up with **teenagers wanting the keys to the car.** This gentle and humorous analogy said it perfectly. They were ready for more autonomy. I will always remember that team as the kids wanting the keys to the car.

Different systems also have different levels of developmental evolution. Many of us have worked at companies that felt almost reptilian. Such companies compete (hostile takeovers, fighting over market shares) and excrete (pollution and fraud). Other organizations may have a deep concern for society and for their employees. What developmental level is your company? Reptilian, mammalian, primate? What does that metaphor mean to you?

WHY DOES THE PRINCIPLE OF UNIQUENESS MATTER?

Relationship Systems have their own strengths, weaknesses, character, and purpose. Each system has something different to sharpen our Relationship Systems Intelligence. When we join a large organization, especially one that is important to us, it begins to shape us to fit into its own unique culture. We unconsciously adapt to its vocabulary and language. We learn about its values, what is important and what isn't. We learn how to fit in.

If you are searching for a new job, you may have come across company websites that describe themselves as "like a family" on the "About" page of their website. For some of us, that description can raise the hair on the back of the neck! The last thing we want is for our company to be like our family of origin! Yet, like a family, every company's culture **will** shape its employees. What happens if that company culture is unhealthy or even corrupt?

When the Enron scandal broke in 2001, thousands of people lost billions of dollars in pensions and stocks. The world was left wondering how the seventh biggest company in the US was able to fall apart overnight.[29] Described by former executive Sherron Watkins as having a culture of

---

29 If you're interested in learning more about the Enron scandal, we'd recommend "Enron: The Smartest Guys in the Room," a documentary about the rise and fall of the company, as well as the key players responsible for the scandal.

arrogance and intimidation, Enron offers us a great example of how company cultures can shape us, for better or for worse.

Deeper analysis of the scandal has revealed a dysfunctional corporate culture that encouraged employees to push limits. Writing for the Wall Street Journal *in 2002, Raghavan, Kranhold, and Barrionuevo described Enron as pushing "everything to the limits:" business practices, laws, and personal behavior. A 2020* Harvard Business Review *article, "Overconfidence Is Contagious," goes as far as to write that many of Enron's employees "felt like they were part of an elite group and believed they were smarter than everybody else."*

Enron, of course, is a well-known cautionary tale for how a predatory company can subvert the behavior of its employees. Human beings are social animals; we adapt to fit in. We long to be "in" with the cool kids. And the larger the system, the more likely the culture of that system will shape us.

Of course, organizations can also promote positive cultures. Coaches and consultants know that culture can be created consciously and intentionally. One way to do this is to look for company values that are behaviorally lived rather than being a dusty mission statement on the wall. CRR Global teaches a wealth of RSI techniques to support healthy engagement and positivity. We know that all cultures can be shaped.

We can easily see this in family systems as well. At age four, I was in a store with my mother, and I took a lollipop and walked out with it. My mother noticed and said firmly, "That is stealing! We do **not** steal things in this family." She marched me back into the store and made me give the lollipop back and apologize for stealing. At age four, I wasn't even clear what stealing was, but the experience was searing for me. I never stole anything again. When adolescent friends indulged in a little light shoplifting, all I could hear was my mum's voice, "We do **not** steal things in this family." My mother was teaching me the cultural code of my family.

CREATING A UNIQUE FAMILY CULTURE-THURSDAY NIGHT SEMINAR

When it comes to parenting there are probably easier ways to develop your unique family culture. We would like to offer one exercise that we call Thursday night seminars.

One evening a week, have a real and important topic of conversation with your family during dinner. Any family member (adult or child) can volunteer the topic, but in the discussion, everyone's opinions are heard and respected. The topic may be a news event, a school incident, or a moral issue. Topics may be very simple: "Vanna said I was stupid at school." The topic is then explored by everyone at the table. Kids can speak freely, but adults can **only** ask questions.

Adult: "Why did she call you stupid?"
Six-year-old: "Well, Sally usually plays with Vanna, but now Sally wants to play with me. So, I think Vanna's mad."
Adult: "What did you do when she called you a name?"
Six-year-old: "I said no, **she** was stupid."
Adult: "How did that work out for the two of you?"
Six-year-old: "I don't know. She won't talk to me now."
Adult (addressing the fourteen-year-old daughter at the table): "Letitia, what do you think about that?"
Fourteen-year-old: "Oh please, this is baby stuff."
Adult: "What, is there no name-calling in high school?"
Fourteen-year-old: "Well, not like that."
Adult: "Why do you think people call each other names?"
Fourteen-year-old: "They call you a name when they want to be mean, and they don't know what else to say."

From here, the conversation can be further explored through questions. When an issue is explored using questions and the child's response is respected, it supports their own moral development. I will never forget the time that Erin, my thirteen-year-old vegetarian daughter, refused to do a fetal pig dissection in biology class. It was a laboratory requirement, and she told her teacher it went against her beliefs. We discussed it during one of our Thursday night seminars, and she said it was wrong and inconsistent with her vegetarian values. (It should be noted that the rest of the family was **not** vegetarian. That was the topic of many other seminars!)

We also explored the scholastic consequences she would face if she didn't complete her biology requirements for the year. She practiced Relationship Warriorship by writing a letter to the Quaker school board stating her beliefs and her position as a conscientious objector to the fetal pig dissection. To the school's credit, they honored her request. Her biology teacher worked out a different project for her to complete that didn't involve cutting open a dead baby pig. To this day, my daughter has a well-developed moral sense (often different from mine), and she has vivid memories of our Thursday night seminar conversations.

TIPS FOR THURSDAY NIGHT SEMINARS

- Adults should only use open-ended questions. Avoid steering the conversation by saying, "Don't you think it's wrong to call people names?"

- Do not use the seminars as a bully pulpit to preach your values. It is a parent's job to promote family values, but not during Thursday night seminars! On those evenings, you are building Relationship Warriorship discernment in the family. Seminars are to support kids in developing a respectful analysis of the topic, thinking critically, and forming an informed opinion. The seminars aid the **vertical** development of your child's emotional intelligence. What do they believe? What are their values, and why are they important? You are also building Relationship Systems Intelligence. How should they proceed at school? What actions do they want to take about what they believe? This promotes horizontal development, the social tools and skills needed to be successful in relating with others.

- Seminars model how to have a respectful disagreement of values. The fact that Erin was a vegetarian when the rest of us were not meant extra work for me. She often helped to prepare her own meals to make it easier.

- It allows for a judgment-free space for the parent to share their own childhood experiences, as long as it is not pushing a point.

- Keep the topic and questions age-appropriate. The topic of abortion is not appropriate to explore with a small child, but it is appropriate to explore with a teen.

- Thursday night seminars develop the Relationship Systems Intelligence of your family on every systemic level. "What do I believe?" builds the ME system. "How am I different or the same as my sister?" builds the YOU/ME system. "How do I deal with the larger systems I am a part of?" builds the WE system. "Do I have the courage and clarity to state my position?" builds Relationship Systems Warriorship. "What tools, skills, and approaches will help me actualize my beliefs" builds RSI.

- Seminars will also provide a treasure trove of information that parents may not always be privy to. To keep the communication open, it's important to accept that your child may sometimes come to a decision that you do not approve of. Your six-year-old may say, "I called her a name because she deserved it! I'm not sorry!" That is your child's truth in that moment; don't try to talk her out of her feelings. The seminar is a safe space to hear your child's experience, if only for one night a week. If you are worried about her response, you can take it up with her on a different night. Seminar night is a safe space for kids to be honest and build their Relationship Warriorship.

- The seminar is a boundaried space with its own agreements. Develop ground rules with your kids, and remember they get to bring their own concerns about the experience. They may say, "I can't be honest! I was honest last week, and later, you came and wanted to 'talk.'" Boom! As a parent, you're busted. Your kids will not open up about what they really feel if they think you are waiting to pounce on them. However, the exchange **is** a golden doorway to the next seminar topic, which could include topics like trust, the role of the parent, different rules at different times, and changes in your agreements.

Seminars are encounters with your children that create a unique family culture. They bring opportunities to evolve your kids as critical thinkers and people worthy of respect, regardless of age. It develops good citizenship by teaching them to have an opinion, to listen, to develop a voice, and to respect themselves and others. And it teaches parents to listen, consider, respect, and manage judgment about their kids. We believe small exercises like this help to build responsible citizens who are thoughtful, engaged, and skillful.

WHY THE PRINCIPLE OF UNIQUENESS IS IMPORTANT FOR EVOLUTION

Every relationship system you encounter, whether it's your family, your leadership team, or your golfing group, is unique in its character. As a boss or a consultant, just because one approach worked with one team is no guarantee that the same approach will work with the next. Right Relationship with each system will be different. Some useful things to remember:

- Learn the ways that each system is unique. The metaphor game is useful for this. Meet the system by taking the time to know who is standing in front of you and what their history is. For example, at CRR Global, we are working with our own systemic equity issues. Black Lives Matter is a critical movement for addressing systemic racism in the United States. But we also know from our international partners that the issues of racism in Europe and Asia are very different. Each region has its own unique system with its own unique diversity issues.

- Meet each system where they are. Working with systems teaches us to be nimble. What worked before may not work again. Here is an example.

We often use a playful, light, and lively exercise called, "What I like about that is . . ." One person starts a story or shares an opinion, sometimes quite outrageous. They hand off to their partner, who picks up the dialogue beginning with the statement, "What I like about that is . . ." before taking the story in another direction.

Park Naturalist #1 – "I think we are getting fewer cougar cubs this year because the parents are harassed by too many tourists."

Park Naturalist #2 – "What I like about that is that we could start advocating to block access to areas where there are cougar lairs. Or we could feed a few tourists to the cougars."

Park Naturalist #1 (laughing) – "What I like about that is it would also provide a bigger food source for the cubs. We could do a lottery at the park entrance. If you win the lottery, you are fed to the cougars."

Park Naturalist #2 – "What I like about that is that is we could do a whole PR event around "support your local cougars, be a food source."

We use this exercise because it is silly, playful, and creates positivity. It helps people practice letting go of their personal position long enough to try on another person's (possibly crazy) viewpoint. We use it to help teams to move out of advocacy and into inquiry. One day, we tried the exercise with a group of scientists at a large national park. We barely got through two rounds of "What I like about that . . ." before the group rebelled. For them, finding a way to appreciate something about an opinion you might not agree with was not in scientific integrity. The scientific method was based on respectful critique! Pretending to agree with something was unprofessional. Scientific integrity trumped cognitive flexibility for them. We had successfully used this light and lively exercise dozens of times with teams. But it nearly tanked our coaching with this particular client!

HAVING HEART FOR EVERY UNIQUE SYSTEM

There is another great reason to get curious about the unique system standing in front of you. It will make your connection to them much more enjoyable. Think of every family or team standing in front of you as a vivid, quirky Third Entity, like a slightly eccentric uncle. The world has arranged for them to come into your life for some reason. You have something to teach them, and they have something to teach you. Understanding each system as a unique entity can give you a slight remove, a gentle distance that lets you see them more clearly and allows you to take things less personally. It provides you with an overview of that system. At the very least, you can get curious about them and enjoy the ride.

There is a secret about working with relationship systems. To truly work effectively with a team, it helps to find something you can love about them. *But wait a minute, isn't that word "love" unprofessional?* Oh please, when did caring and affection become unprofessional? When working with a stressed-out relationship system, we need heartfelt connection more than we need remote professionalism. Being heartfelt is as important as professional skills because your teams and families will feel it. Can you love the enthusiastic chaos of a start-up, long on passion and short on experience? Can you sit with the pain of a company that is going bankrupt and help its employees find dignity and meaning in its ending? Can you be in the fire with a family that is consuming itself with a divorce? When we encounter a system, we enter into a relationship with it. We need all our education, tools, and skills, but Relationship Warriors also need to have heart. It's very hard to work with a team or a family that we just don't like. Our judgment and disdain will flavor our interactions with them. Can you find something you love about this unique family, this eccentric team, or this quirky non-profit?

We have such a limited story about what "love" and "intimacy" can mean. We'd like to start a movement for creating more heart in business. In coaching, we sometimes say coaching is about seeing the beauty in your client and being fierce in championing that beauty. If that is not part of loving your clients, then I don't know what is! We take for granted that we love our family, but what if we had the same heartfelt commitment to our teams? What if we truly cared about them and their well-being?

If we are going to have more "heart," we must allow our emotions to inform us as well as our professional acumen. This is still a huge edge for coaches, consultants, and managers. Yet, emotions and intuition are legitimate assessment tools in working with a company. By excluding emotions from "professionalism," we have cut ourselves off from a big area of information. How we feel about a system tells us a lot about ourselves and about them. Granted, this is easier to do in intimate relationships and more difficult when we have a professional role (CEO, coach, etc.). Heart means letting ourselves **feel** something about a system. Does the team irritate us? What does that feeling teach us about ourselves? Do they threaten us? Why is that? Does the team touch a tender spot in us? Be curious. Whatever you are feeling, it is likely that they have that impact on others as well. Can we give ourselves over to an emotional connection without losing all our objectiveness? Do we even want "objectiveness" in every situation? Perhaps we have gone too far in the direction of professionalism.

RELATIONSHIP WARRIORSHIP EXERCISE: MEETING YOUR SYSTEMS – THE METAPHOR GAME

Describe your team or family as if they are a unique character. Come up with a metaphor for them. Would they be a person, animal, vegetable, or an object? Then start asking questions:

- In your imagination, do they have a particular age or sex? Color or movement?

- If they wore an outfit, what would it be?

- What are they good at?

- How does it feel when you're with them? Do they feel disengaged or withdrawn?

- Are they firing people? Do they fight all the time?

- What does their metaphor express for the whole company or family?

- What do you love about them?

- What are they teaching you?

- Are you willing to tell them this? How might that open up a conversation? What gets in the way of you communicating your experience of them?

CHAPTER 13

PRINCIPLE – SYSTEMS ARE IN A CONSTANT STATE OF EMERGENCE

SYSTEMS ARE IN CONSTANT STATE OF EMERGENCE

FUTURE

PAST

"Sometimes I go about feeling sorry for myself when the whole time I am being blown across the sky by a great wind."

– OBJIBWAY PROVERB

"Life is a series of natural and spontaneous changes. Don't resist them; that only creates sorrow. Let reality be reality. Let things flow naturally forward in whatever way they like."

– LAO TZU

CHANGE IS CONSTANT

Emergence is the pattern that arises via the collective actions of many individual entities. In Buddhism, one of the first noble truths is impermanence. We don't have to be Buddhist to appreciate this. Nothing in life stays the same. Change is constant, and the emergence of the new is happening every moment. This is one of the most basic systemic principles, applicable to having a baby, to economic recession, or to new disease vectors. Emergence shows up in our minds in the flow of our thoughts or a new solution to a problem. It arises in life events: getting married, a business bankruptcy, or a school shooting. And, of course, it is literally happening on a cosmic level, as galaxies collide, and stars explode. No single event is causative; it is a complex, interactive dance of multiple factors. For individuals, the ME system is emergent as events and relationships mold our character. As partnerships, we will shape each other personally and relationally. Teams, organizations, and countries are impacted by countless vectors like market forces, wars, and climate change. Whether we like it or not, we are in constant partnership with emergence. The one thing we can control is our response to it.

EVERY SYSTEM IS CONSTANTLY EVOLVING IN ITS OWN LIFE CYCLE

All Relationship Systems have a birth, a period of growth, occasional illness, and a death. The lifecycle of an organization may last for a hundred years or longer. In the process, it will grow and change itself repeatedly to adapt to new circumstances. Most entities will eventually die or change to something radically different from where they started. Certainly, this is true for families. The family line may continue, but each generation must pass away. This is the natural lifecycle of relationship systems and a normal one. If we want to work effectively with an organization or a family, we need to appreciate where it is in its lifecycle.

How do we help a family to absorb the death of a patriarch? Or help a company to move past the retirement of a founder? How do we help a closing organization to honor its past and harvest its learnings? Sometimes our best efforts fail because the next step in the journey of that system is to dissolve. When we are attached to a particular outcome, it is hard to be with what is. Can we still serve the system in its death, failure, or dissolution?

Emergence is an invitation from the universe to participate in it. We are a creation of our genes, our decisions, our family, our circumstances, and our society. All these factors and hundreds more shape what we are becoming.

Of course, this is also true for businesses.

CRR Global is an international training company. Our skilled faculty are trained to create an engaged, intimate, live classroom experience. However, in March 2020, the COVID-19 pandemic emerged. Face-to-face classes shut down all over the globe. Like everyone else in the world, CRR cycled wildly between feeling empowered—"We could go virtual!"—and feeling totally helpless—"What if people don't want virtual courses?" The timespan for meaningful planning was narrowed down to about a month. Was COVID-19 going to disappear "like a miracle," as the US President declared?[30] How were our partners in different countries handling the pandemic? We had so many questions and so few answers. After about a month of shocked paralysis, we realized we would be dead in the water if we didn't convert our courses to a virtual format. The pandemic was emergent, but we could dance with it. We virtualized all our courses within six months, and today we remain a viable company.

Emergence upsets the apple cart. For some industries, it can be the kiss of death. For our industry, it has been a midwife to constructive change. The pandemic forced us to become creative and adaptive at a startling speed. Things that would have taken months or years to accomplish during "normal" times happened in weeks. We all have examples of surprising ways different companies have adapted—or not—to the shocking emergence of a pandemic.

"If you trust that something is trying to emerge through you, then you don't feel so alone. Lean into what it is that wants to be expressed through you."

– CRR GLOBAL

---

30 Since the start of the coronavirus outbreak, President Trump repeatedly said that the virus would disappear, (Vazquez & Kelly, 2020).

Emergence isn't just about concrete events. It's also a psychological phenomenon. In an earlier chapter, we talked about how Cantor Fitzgerald responded to the destruction of their team during 9/11, a classic, uncontrollable, emergent event. Cantor found a way to channel their pain into supporting the families of the victims. However, when dealing with a devastating event, it's easy to forget that our thoughts and emotions are emerging as well. Shock, grief, and rage (and all the Kübler-Ross states!)[31] emerge one after another, within days or hours. We can't always control how we feel. In 2021, the internet was full of stories about pandemic meltdown. There were days when we lost our focus, our tempers, or something else! This reaction is only natural: an abnormal response to an abnormal situation is normal.

The days that we "lose it" are also an opportunity to learn about ourselves. Sometimes, losing it acts as a simple pressure release when the stress is too intense. It is also an opportunity to get curious. What kinds of situations trigger us? What is the fear behind that trigger? How could I partner better with that fear?

Like it or not, emergence is a midwife to evolution. It forces personal development as we are pushed past the edges of our previous limitations. This is a natural emergence, like the sprouting of an acorn. We can practice Relationship Warriorship with events to shape that emergence collaboratively.

---

31 The five stages of grief model—otherwise known as the Kübler-Ross model—is a framework that helps us to understand the phases of grief. The five stages are denial, anger, bargaining, depression, and acceptance. In her later writings, Kübler-Ross noted that the stages are not a linear, predictable progression. Some have added a sixth stage, "meaning making." To find out more, we'd highly recommend reading *Death and Dying* by Elizabeth Kübler-Ross.

RELATIONSHIP WARRIORSHIP WITH EMERGENCE

So, how **do** we dance with emergence? There is no set of rules, but we do have a few tips. It helps to let go of our fixed view of what is happening. In our intelligence course, we tell the story of the Taoist master who was continuously surprised by the outcome of unexpected events.

When an old farmer's stallion wins a prize at a country show, his neighbor calls to congratulate him, but the old farmer says, "Who knows what is good and what is bad?" The next day some thieves come and steal his valuable animal. His neighbor comes to commiserate with him, but the old man replies, "Who knows what is good and what is bad?" A few days later, the spirited stallion escapes from the thieves and joins a herd of wild mares, leading them back to the farm. The neighbor calls to share the farmer's joy, but the farmer says, "Who knows what is good and what is bad?" The following day, while trying to break in one of the wild mares, the farmer's son is thrown and fractures his leg. The neighbor calls to share the farmer's sorrow, but the old man's attitude remains the same as before. The following week, the army passes by forcibly conscripting soldiers for a war, but they do not take the farmer's son because he cannot walk. The neighbor thinks to himself, "Who knows what is good and what is bad?" and realizes that the old farmer must be a Taoist sage.

- FROM *THE TAO BOOK & CARD PACK* BY TIMOTHY FREKE

"Who knows what is good and what is bad" allows us to have an open mind about the possibilities in any emergent event. Walk the roads of all the possibilities inherent in your situation. Sometimes, even the long arc of destruction eventually creates space for the new to emerge.

To dance with emergence, it also helps to examine the situation through all the systemic lenses: ME, YOU/ME, and WE. Different parts of the system have different perspectives to offer. In the ME system, I may recognize that the emergent situation is triggering me and that I need to work on myself. I can ask myself about the triggering narratives I am telling myself, and what I want to do about that story. Who knows what is good and what is bad?

If I look at the YOU/ME system perspective, I may notice that I'd rather blame my partner than do my own work. For this reason, it is helpful to do the ME work first.

Finally, am I blaming the organizational WE system for being in overwhelm when actually the whole world is in crisis and flooding the emotional field with distress? Are different teams pointing fingers at each other? Each systemic perspective helps us understand a different aspect of what is happening.

RELATIONSHIP WARRIORSHIP EXERCISE: WORKING WITH EMERGENCE

Let's apply the multiple levels of relationship Systems to your own situation. Think of a distressing emergent event in your life.

- What part of the stress emerges from your ME system? Focus on your own EQ. What are the stories you are telling yourself about what happened? What conflicts are happening between the different voices of your ME system?

- What part of your discomfort is coming from your YOU/ME System? How is your narrative about what happened different from the narrative of your partner? Are you feeling the need to blame them or defend yourself? What might be trying to happen between the two of you?

- Are you feeling reactive about something in your WE system? How are larger circumstances impacting your family or your teams? **"Who knows what is good and what is bad?"**

With all this emergence happening, you would think we would be more comfortable with change! But the longing for certainty and stability is literally built into our brains. Predictability gives us a sense of control, and as it happens, our relationship with control profoundly influences our relationship with change.

We can often control some of what is emerging. We can decide whether to start a family or choose a particular career. But whether we actually get pregnant or whether we are accepted at medical school happens in collaboration with the universe. We cannot always control circumstances, but we can often influence them. The moment we are born, we enter the river of time. Our life is basically a journey down that river, experiencing the rapids and still places, enjoying the scenery (or not). We have a paddle, and we do have **some** control, particularly around how we react to the changes on the river. But the river is always moving us along, our past is disappearing behind us, and we never really know what will be around the next bend in the future. Emergence, or complex systemic change, just **is.** Much of our development as a person, a team, or even a country is about how we respond to that change. And how we respond to emergence has a lot to do with our relationship with control. So, now we're going to spend a little bit of time talking about locus of control.

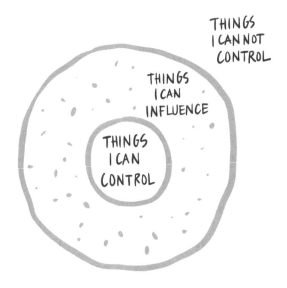

EMERGENCE AND LOCUS OF CONTROL

Locus of Control: "An individual's belief system regarding the causes of his or her experiences and the factors to which that person attributes success or failure."

– PSYCHOLOGY TODAY

The question is, do I believe **I am happening to the world**, or do I believe **the world is happening to me?** The answer to that question profoundly influences our relationship with change. In fact, it influences our relationship with everything.

INTERNAL LOCUS OF CONTROL

"I did it my way."

– FRANK SINATRA

High internal locus of control individuals and systems believe the future will be determined by their own actions. They believe: "I am master of my fate and captain of my destiny." And, of course, some of our understanding of locus of control is cultural.

Western culture is highly invested in control. In the US, the myth of rugged individualism gives rise to a belief that we can wrestle anything in the direction we want it to go. **We** are responsible for making our dreams come true. Western cultures value an internal locus of control, and coaching as a profession is also highly invested in this perspective.

In an article for *Forbes*, Melody Wilding writes that "people who operate with an internal locus of control are more successful in both personal and professional settings—enjoying better health, relationships, and careers."

So, why **wouldn't** we want to strive to look at life through an internal locus of control? Perhaps because it is hard to surrender to what is emergent when we have to control everything!

Internal locus of control systems believe they can predict what is around the next river bend, and they plan for it. This is great, until emergence changes the rules. Twenty-five years ago, there was a strong demand for organizations to develop five-year plans. The belief was that by setting our goals and steering steadfastly towards them, we could better control our organizational destiny. Planning and visioning **is** a very critical organizational skill; nothing can happen without it. Yet, as we move into the mid-2000s, we live in a world characterized by volatility, uncertainty, complexity, and ambiguity (VUCA).[32] The window of reliable future prediction shrinks down to months at best.

Aphorism: *When we make plans, God laughs.*

An additional problem with a high locus of control perspective is that it assumes we are all starting with the same advantages. Yet we know that if we are born poor, black, female, or have a disability, we will encounter certain systemic obstacles on our journey to full self-expression. Are these obstacles insurmountable? Not for some people, but for most, the journey is harder. We do not all start with the same advantages.

EQUALITY   EQUITY

To summarize, internal locus of control gives us the confidence and sense of agency to go for what we want in the world. The disadvantages of internal locus of control include that not everything can be controlled or managed, and we do not all start with the same privileges. This gives rise to the other end of the spectrum.

---

32 VUCA is an acronym short for volatility, uncertainty, complexity, and ambiguity and describes the constant and unpredictable change prevalent in many of today's industries.

EXTERNAL LOCUS OF CONTROL

"Been down so long, it looks like up to me."

– LEE HAZELWOOD, NANCY SINATRA

We have little choice about emergence; the river of change just keeps rolling. However, our stance on locus of control has a lot to do with our ability to engage with it. Systems with an external locus of control often have little sense of their own agency. They believe, often from their life experience, that events are outside their control, and they cannot steer their own life. As the graphic above demonstrates, we do not all start out with the same advantages. After generations of obstacles, it can be hard for marginalized people to feel confident in their futures. Systemic racism, gender bias, ableism, etc., may make us question how much real control we have over our lives. Many of us have lost trust that we can have a collaborative partnership with the emergent.

Marita and Faith were doing coach training for a high-diversity group in a county organization. The topic of systemic racism came up, and one prominent black woman who was the director of a division in the organization told us a story. She lives in a relatively affluent section of town and went with her husband and two little kids to get ice cream one evening. On the way home, they were pulled over by the police, who questioned them about why they were in that area. Her husband explained that they had gone to get ice cream and that they lived right up the street. The police asked to see his license to prove his address, and he carefully complied while the director worked with her kids in the back to stay calm and quiet. Even after her husband had established their address as down the street, the police trailed the car and waited until they unlocked the door.

This was a highly educated woman who was the director of a large agency department. Yet she and her family were profiled and confronted for being black people driving in a largely white neighborhood at night.

Organizations are also struggling with VUCA in current market conditions. We worked with a telecommunication company that was quite successful until the federal communication guidelines changed. New regulations came out that basically paralyzed the company. Even after they had adapted to the new regulations, the company was haunted by the ghost of "this could happen again." Many industries are subject to regulatory changes out of their control. This is true for families as well. Any couple who has suffered a miscarriage knows the fear that accompanies the next pregnancy.

If we have very little control over our lives, we can develop a kind of learned helplessness. "I won't even try because there is no way I can win." When we have been repeatedly blocked or disappointed, we become afraid to try again. It's just too painful. Sometimes, to preserve our self-esteem in organizations, it's just easier to blame others for our failure. "We would have finished that product on time if only **they** (R&D, sales, operations, whomever) had done what they were supposed to!"

Whenever I hear a department complaining about **"they,"** I know I'm dealing with a team struggling with an external locus of control. The world is full of **"theys,"** and obstacles are often real. And it's also possible to hide out in victimization and avoid taking agency for our own performance.

*We were hired to do a relationship course with an aviation manufacturing company, and we were working with the factory floor production team. These were the teams building the actual airplanes. Right away, we noticed that the teams did a lot of complaining about upper management (**they**).*

It was a big organization, so upper management was many hierarchical levels up. The team didn't personally know anyone in upper management. They actually called upper management "the officers," which gives you a feel for the power gap and the military flavor of the management style. The operations teams had a lot of contemptuous complaints about "the officers." Clearly, this team had developed an external locus of control. They had so many layers of management control over them they didn't feel they had the authority to create positive change. We were hired to help them with change, but the team felt helpless to make any changes because they felt that everything was determined by upper management.

Before we could help those teams take more self-authorship, we had to work with that sense of learned helplessness. We started by asking them, **"What do you want?"** *To our surprise, it was a surprisingly difficult question for them to answer. Assuming they had no power, they hadn't gotten concrete about the changes they wanted. For a period, we went through cycles of: "What's the use of wanting anything? We can't determine anything anyway." Unfortunately, an internal locus of control also means assuming responsibility for what happens to us. If we want things to be different, it is up to us to start. Sometimes, it is just easier not to make the effort. "Well, there is nothing we can do about it, so don't even try." Having a high level of internal locus of control is actually a lot of work! We become responsible for what happens in our life. If we fail, it is on us. Am I willing to take that kind of personal responsibility for my life? It takes energy and resilience and the serenity prayer[33] to develop a strong internal locus of control.*

So, what happened to the engineering team struggling with management? It took time for the production teams to develop the confidence to

---

33 *God grant me the courage to change the things I can*
The serenity to accept the things I can't
And the wisdom to know the difference.

go for the changes they wanted. We kept asking them what they wanted and working through their sense of "it's no use" until, finally, they created a list of things they would ask for. Once they could say what they wanted, we moved them to the locus of control exercise listed below. Which requests were in their control (inside the donut), and which requests might be open to influence? Which ones were outside their control? Finally, they had a well-thought-out list of the requests to take to the next level of management.

Did they get what they wanted? Well, they were able to get **some** of what they wanted, not **all** of what they wanted. But the team had acted for themselves, which helped to undo that sense of learned helplessness. They now knew that they could indeed create some changes **if** they were willing to take a stand for what they wanted.

Below is an example of using the locus of control exercise with this production team.

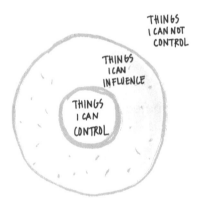

Things the production team can control would include:

- Getting clear on what changes we need.

- Taking action to ask for what we want.

- Creating a plan for presenting these changes in an effective way to upper management.

- Not giving up.

- Organizing with other production teams to present a united front.

In the donut part of the graphic, they worked on **things we can influence.** Some of their examples were:

- Consulting with our immediate bosses on the best way to present our case for the change

- Making a dollars and cents business case for the changes

- Prioritizing the most important changes if we cannot get all of them

- If we get a no, ask what we would need to change to get a yes

- Getting influential allies to support the change

- Working with our own negative attitude about the officers to create a more collaborative approach

- Getting educated about relevant budgetary priorities that could affect our requests

Outside of the donut is labeled **things we cannot control.** It has examples like:

- Budget restraints

- Competing organizational needs

- Market changes

The most interesting part of this exercise is sorting what belongs in what part of the donut. For example, the team initially felt that they had **no** control over whether the Officers said yes or no. But on examination, there were a lot of things they could influence. When we do this exercise, often the bulk of factors lie within the influenceable region. Emotional factors should also be considered. We all have some control over our emotional experiences. How did the team want to deal with their own low locus of control? How easily would they give up? How does their contempt for management impact their ability to be effective?

Now, let's give you the opportunity to try it out.

RELATIONSHIP WARRIORSHIP EXERCISE: LOCUS OF CONTROL

You will need two pieces of paper and a pencil.

- Think of a complex situation you are in that perhaps is making you anxious. Write the topic at the top of your paper.

- Draw a large slim donut shape on your paper. Give yourself plenty of room.

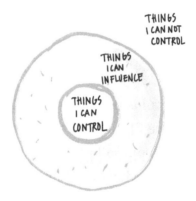

- In the center of your donut hole, write down all the things you know you can control (strong internal locus of control).

- In the cake part of the donut, write down all the things you can influence. Influence gives you some locus of control over what happens. Make sure to include psychological events like feelings as well. I cannot control the fact that I lost a contract, but I can influence my reactions to losing that contract.

- Outside the donut, write down all the things that you cannot control (external locus of control).

- Question: which part of the donut are you spending the most time worrying about? Are you spending a lot of energy on things you cannot control? It is much more useful to think about the things you can influence or control.

- Choose one or two issues you can influence or control and make a short plan for how you will work with them. Again, consider psychological and relationship issues as well. You may not be able to control the reactions of others, but you may be able to influence them. Emotions can usually be worked with or mediated in some way. What is your plan?

- This exercise can also be used with families who are struggling with an emergent event like a layoff.

An external locus of control is not necessarily bad. If we are caught in an inevitable circumstance like a natural disaster or a terminal illness, an external locus of control may allow us to surrender to circumstances rather than battling them. It helps to have a flexible locus of control responsive to the situation. In any situation, there are usually a few things I can control, some things I cannot control, but quite a few that I can influence.

WHY IS THE PRINCIPLE OF EMERGENCE IMPORTANT TO HUMAN EVOLUTION?

"Between stimulus and response there is a space. In that space is our power to choose our response. In our response lies our growth and our freedom."

– VICTOR FRANKL

All the principles are important, yet emergence is probably the most impactful in terms of shaping our growth as human beings. Our ability to dance with change defines who we are as a person, as a spouse, and as a leader. Can you and I allow the universe to co-create with us? To do this requires Relationship Warriorship.

The evolutionary skill of working with emergence is learning to listen to the many factors influencing the system. **Rather than who is doing what to whom, what is trying to happen?** What is trying to happen with the ME system, the YOU/ME system, and the WE system? We will grow alongside the emergent as we learn to dance with it. Can we lead but also follow when circumstances suggest a new way? Emergence is the principle that opens us up to grace in our lives; the give and take, the flow and surrender.

RELATIONSHIP WARRIORSHIP EXERCISE: THE IMPACT OF EMERGENCE THROUGH RELATIONSHIP SYSTEMS

- ME System: Write down personal transformations, traumas, and experiences that have shaped you into who you are today. How did they influence your own emergence?

- YOU/ME: Write down some of the history and the ups and downs that have shaped your close relationships. In what way did those events influence the relationship?

- WE: Think of your business or extended family. What triumphs and failures have informed it? How is it different from what you thought your business or family would be like?

- In what way have emergent events shaped your leadership style? Write it down.

- Notice if events in one level of your life have impacted another system. A bankruptcy may impact your marriage. A new baby may impact your business.

CHAPTER 14

PRINCIPLE – EVERY MEMBER OF A RELATIONSHIP SYSTEM IS A VOICE OF THE SYSTEM (VOS)

EVERY MEMBER OF A
RELATIONSHIP SYSTEM IS
A VOICE OF THE SYSTEM

The image we use for the Principle of the voice of the system is a jazz band. Each player makes a unique contribution to the song. Every instrument is needed to complete the piece.

When we talk about the multiple entities within a systems approach, people sometimes say, "What about the importance and impact of specific people in the team? One person can dominate a whole team." This is true! Individuals do have an important impact on every family and team. A single bully can make working in a department an absolute misery. A powerful leader can change the course of a company. So, we are a big **yes** to the power of the individual. Individuals hold a dual role in the system. They are both their own self (ME), and they are a voice expressing their unique viewpoint of the system (WE). The self is the first system, and every person benefits from understanding their own internal voices, skills, and liabilities. Similarly, it is the differences between the individual partners that often force a YOU/ME relationship to grow. There are many times that one partner makes a change that impacts the Third Entity of the couple.

For example, initially, Marita and I worked together from a psychotherapeutic perspective. Then, she trained to become a coach. In her excitement about the new coaching tools, she advocated that we use them in our next team gig. I was not familiar with these tools, so this threw our professional Third Entity into short-term chaos. She had crossed a developmental edge that I had not. Once I saw the power of the tools, I also got coach training, and the rest is history. Marita's evolution, her voice, forced us both to grow personally and professionally.

This is how YOU/ME systems grow, one partner crosses an edge, and the other follows. When working with larger companies or families, we want to pay attention to individual work and pairs work, and we also want to expand to a larger systemic perspective, the collective (WE). The Third Entity of an organization is formed by the members who are part of it.

Its character will change over time as its members come and go, so we value the contribution of **every** person in that family or team as a voice of that particular system. The only way a family or team system can express itself is through the voices of its members. Individuals are literally how the system speaks its views.

In the individual system (the ME), all my different voices don't always get along. In the same way, the different voices within larger WE systems may not always be aligned.

Yet, it is through the voices of each family member that the family system can express itself. Each family member has their own unique experience that is also an expression of the overall system.

Three generations of a family were planning on moving to Israel. The father of the family had been offered a job promotion in Israel, and the parents jumped at the chance to deepen the family's Jewish identity. The family consisted of a set of grandparents in their seventies, two teenagers, and a nine-year-old. Each generation of the family had a different voice about the move.

- *The parents were excited and pushing for the move, "What an opportunity!"*

- *The grandparents were anxious. "We're not sure we are up for such a big change at our age." Yet they didn't want to be left behind.*

- *The teenagers were flat out against the move. "You're going to ruin our lives!" They wanted to stay in their high school with their friends and their extracurricular activities. They didn't want to miss their prom, leave their boyfriends, etc. To them, the move felt disruptive and disrespectful to their needs.*

● *The nine-year-old was excited about the adventure of living in a new country. "It's awesome. Wait till I tell them at school!"*

Each viewpoint makes sense from the perspective of the individuals. Naturally, their response would be shaped by their age and developmental level. However, from the systemic level, each person was also expressing something important for the family's Third Entity. The grandparents carried some of the anxiety for everyone in the family. Everyone had a part of themselves that worried about how they would fit in with the new culture and felt exhausted at the prospect of such a big move. The teenagers carried the voice of everyone's resentment at leaving their lives and losing their friends and identity. The nine-year-old was in touch with the excitement of the adventure of it all. Were all these issues individual? Yes, of course, but each person was also an expression of all the different feelings that the family Third Entity was having at the prospect of the move. Their different concerns were personal but also systemic. It was important to validate and hear the different generations individually. And certainly, the family did a lot of work to address everyone's real concerns.

*However, when we hold each person as **a voice of the system**, each person's perspective is generalized and empowered. Instead of focusing on the teens as "the obstructing kids," we could suggest that they were representing something important for the whole family. We could discuss how everyone in the family was going to miss friends and important activities. It was more than a teenage problem; it was a systemic issue. Rather than glossing over the grandparents' anxiety, we could have the whole family discuss their worries about the new culture, medical care, etc. We could tap into the nine-year-old's sense of adventure for everyone. When someone's voice is honored as an important expression of the whole system, we are all less likely to brace against a particular viewpoint. **Everyone's experience is partially right**.*

When we move out of advocating for one particular position and move into curiosity for another's position, then it becomes possible to pool our collective intelligence. We can collaboratively problem-solve. No particular person is the "identified patient."[34] They are each expressing a systemic perspective like different instruments in a band. When we recognize that every voice is an expression of the system, we move out of the protective **"but what about ME"** position to **"how is this issue impacting us all."** Decisions still have to be made, but they can be held within a larger collective understanding.

DEEP DEMOCRACY

When we are willing to listen to each entity as a voice of the system, we are practicing the evolutionary tool of Deep Democracy.

Deep Democracy: This term was coined by Arnie and Amy Mindell. Practicing deep democracy means that ALL the voices in a system need to be heard if we are to accurately represent the reality of that system. We cannot know the truth of a system until everyone's perspective is understood. This especially includes voices that may be disturbing or uncomfortable.

Like a chorus, every voice in the system carries an important piece of information that we ignore at our peril. If the teens were simply strong-armed into moving to Israel, the decision would be simpler. And the kids might move there and love it. But ignoring their concerns and needs could

---

34 Identified patient (IP) is a clinical term often used in family therapy discussion. It describes one family member in a dysfunctional family who expresses the family's authentic inner conflicts.

also set up the family to live with big resentments and stress. Discussing the teens' social needs brought up deeper systemic issues. If the family lived in Israel, would the kids grow up with an American identity? How did the parents feel about their kids potentially becoming more Israeli than American? What starts as an adolescent rebellion about missing high school prom turns out to be a much bigger discussion about values and identity. The teens are a critical voice of the system.

The family created an honest container for everyone in the family to be heard and to give input into the process. When they made the actual move, there was still plenty of anxiety and resistance floating around. At the same time, they had more trust and confidence in their own ability to work through their issues together.

The principle of the voice of the system is also critical for organizations.

Even unpleasant voices can point out important truths.

 ## THE BEACH MASTER

We once worked with a management team of a small IT company. We were hired to develop leadership skills for the whole team, but an assessment of the company indicated that there was a VP of sales who was a bully. Other teammates reported that she was aggressive, abusive, and domineering. Several people on her own team had chosen to leave the company rather than continue to work with her. And behind her back, the rest of the team called her the beach master. A beach master is a name given to a several-ton apex male sea lion who bellows up and down the beach, attacking other male sea lions to protect his territory. Clearly, the team viewed the VP as constantly throwing her weight around aggressively.

As the team reviewed the assessment information together, the VP lost her temper. "I know you guys can't stand my style. I know you call me the beach master. Do you think I like that? Well, I'll tell you this . . . I'm the only one who speaks up on this team when there's a problem. You guys won't do a thing."

She then swung around to face the CEO: "You have made me your attack dog. Whenever something unpleasant comes up, you send me out to do your dirty work, so you don't have to deal with unpleasantness. You may not like me, but you use me . . . and I'm not crazy about that. I may not be popular, but my sales team has had the highest profits of anyone here because I won't tolerate non-performance."

After a stunned silence, we all needed time to regroup, especially the facilitators! We took a fifteen-minute break and asked the group to reflect on what they had heard. Something big, ugly, and important had just been revealed. The hostile VP was operating as a voice of the system.

When we came back, the CEO stepped into his Relationship Warriorship and admitted there was some truth in what the VP said, "You're right, I don't like conflict, and you don't mind it, so sometimes I delegate conflicts for you to handle. You've never told me you felt used by that. But delegating to you has led to some real HR messes as well. It's true, you have the best sales team. You are so effective at sales that, frankly, I didn't want to rock the boat. But your style also comes at a high human resources cost."

We later worked with the CEO and VP privately to change their agreements. But the VP had revealed something else that needed to be addressed with the rest of the management team. She had blown the cover on the team's relationship with conflict. She **was** the only one willing to deal with conflict while everyone else avoided it. Part of her role was to give tough feedback to people who had a performance problem. She was very unskillful in her actions, but she was willing to say unpleasant truths and get rid of anyone who didn't live up to her expectations.

We started asking the team some difficult questions. Everyone was privately complaining about the VP's behavior behind her back, but no one had *confronted her. Why was that? Why had they not brought the bullying issue up more forcefully with the CEO? Why did they tolerate her bad behavior, and how did they benefit from it? Was it possible that they were colluding with the beach master for her to carry all the negativity for the team? We also needed to have a frank conversation about the company culture and values. Did profitability trump a respectful culture? Were they mutually exclusive? What were the companywide expectations in terms of performance? What were their agreements about how to handle conflict? The VP was a voice of the system, and she revealed many important things about her team.*

- *Part of her role was to be the voice expressing the anger and negativity repressed by the rest of the team. She unskillfully revealed the system's discomfort with conflict.*

- *Because her Relationship Systems Intelligence was low, she was toxic in her style. She was unskillful in her delivery, but she was the one person demanding and getting high sales performance, which was keeping the company afloat.*

- *She uncovered the way she was used by the CEO to deal with difficult confrontations that he did not like to do.*

The VP was a complex individual with a deep comfort with confrontation but an unfortunate style of expressing it. Did she need individual work? Yes, absolutely. Her manner was destructive. However, she was also a voice of the system, revealing the team's conflict avoidance.

Every individual in the system is a voice of the system. What they have to say represents some characteristic of it. Is every voice the truth? No. Every voice is **one** experiential truth about the situation. Each voice is like a band member. Each one has one piece of reality. By tapping into each perspective, you can start to get the bigger picture of the status of the team, company, or family on a particular topic.

Deep Democracy is the Relationship Systems Intelligence skill associated with this principle. As a leader or as a family member, it is important to hear all the different voices in the system. *"Wait a minute. Does this mean that every voice is equal?"* No. Some voices have more weight than others do. Hierarchy and rank are a fact in any system. When considering a new client management system, the voice of the CEO carries more weight than the data entry person. However, the CEO needs to hear the perspective of the data entry personnel because they carry technical experience on what works and what doesn't.

WHY THE PRINCIPLE OF VOICE OF THE SYSTEM IS IMPORTANT TO RELATIONSHIP EVOLUTION

It is human nature to advocate for ME, my position, my needs, and my beliefs, particularly in Western countries. Some of the primary Western values include freedom of choice, individual rights, and independence. A narrow interpretation of this perspective can lead to social irresponsibility when the rights of the ME trump the rights of the WE. To stay locked into our limited perspective of ME is to refuse to open up to critical information. No single person has all the information we need to navigate in this VUCA era. We all have blind spots. We need all the knowledge we can get. Much of that knowledge lives in the other parts of the system. We need to at least hear all those perspectives in order to make an informed decision. As a society, we need deep democracy to understand the impact of any choice. Below is a story that our faculty member Jim Patterson loved to talk about when he worked for the Peace Corps.

*Jim's team was charged with creating a well for an African village. The women of the village had to walk several miles to get water from the river, which was very time-consuming. The work team was able to drill for water in the very heart of the village and soon put in a beautiful new well that everyone could access easily. The problem was the women continued to walk the long road to the river together and ignored the well. It turns out the walk to the river was **women's time**, the opportunity for them to talk and socialize away from the other demanding chores of the day. The shiny new well did not give them that critical relationship time. The team focused on convenience without uncovering the deeper values of the walk to the river. They hadn't talked enough to the women.*

Listening to all the voices of the system also empowers the engagement and leadership of everyone. The adolescents in the family moving to Israel felt seen when they realized their issues were heard and might be relevant to the rest of the family. One of the best ways to get people engaged on a topic is to **ask** people for their opinion and really listen to them. This does not mean agreeing with it; it means considering the input useful for its own sake.

There are usually secret truths underneath the initial issue. The beach master was a disturber for the team; it was easy to make her the problem. But when her perspective was opened up, there were difficult truths the entire team needed to address. She was a signal for a deeper conflict issue that needed to be addressed by everyone.

Finally, listening to the voices of the system also safeguards information. Critical systemic information will recycle if you don't hear it the first time. That is the good news and the bad news. When working with a team, sometimes we worry that we will miss something important that is under the surface. And we will miss things. But if we do, that issue will just keep cropping up repeatedly until we get the message. The system **will** be heard on important issues. Topics will just keep repeating until they are heard.

Deep Democracy helps us to grow as a person and a community when we identify with ever larger systemic entities. When I am a baby, there is only myself, my hunger, my needs. As I grow up, I learn that others in the family have their own needs. Eventually, I identify with my schoolmates, community, profession, teams, organization, and country. I learn to grow in my empathetic awareness of others. As we evolve, we become more and more aware of the many voices that make up society. We stretch to hold more and more subjective "truths" within us. The more we can empathize with others, the less certain we are about our precious convictions. We learn to include and transcend rather than going either/or. The **WE** has become as important as the **ME**.

Deep Democracy is a critical skill for working with highly charged situations. At CRR Global, we do not presume to have the answers for how to resolve the extreme political splits seen around the globe at this time. But we do have a sense of where to begin. We must be able to listen to one another and be curious. Why does this person believe what they believe? Even if we think they are crazy, why is it important for them to believe that? What are the drivers, the fears, and the values behind their position? What do they long for? Can we go for understanding **why** this position is important to them rather than trying to change their mind? Can we put the problem out in front and look at it together?

I once had such a conversation with someone of very different political views. We both kept digging deep. Nope, we did not change each other's beliefs one inch. But we both left the conversation feeling heard. There was an appreciation that these very different people had just spent nearly two hours trying to understand each other. We cared enough to try to connect and understand. **It's not just about the outcome; it's about relationship.** Conversations like this may not move the political goalpost. But a sense of common relationship undercuts the contempt, fear, and antipathy that can make these exchanges so deeply polarizing.

"But isn't holding all those voices paralyzing? How do I ever make a decision?" On the other side of the spectrum, we also need to decide where we draw a boundary. Connecting with people very different from ourselves can be exhausting! Relationship Warriorship can only take us so far before our own integrity of character starts to tear. Can I stretch to understand the experience of another race, class, or gender? Where does my ability to incorporate the experience of others hit a limit? How do I balance my personal beliefs with the moral relativism of my expanded perspective? There is no easy answer to this, but from the Relationship Warrior perspective, struggling with these questions forces us to grow.

RELATIONSHIP WARRIORSHIP EXERCISE

What are my system limits?

- Where does your ability to empathize with another's behavior or belief grind to a halt?

- What is it that you make up about that person (or collective), that makes it a road too far for you to understand their experience?

- What are you afraid might happen if you totally empathized with their experience?

CHAPTER 15

PRINCIPLE – SYSTEMS ARE NATURALLY INTELLIGENT, CREATIVE, AND GENERATIVE

CRR Global is an ICF Approved Coach Training Program (ACTP). As a certified program, we are bound by the ethics and principles of the coaching profession. One of the most central principles of coaching is holding the client as intelligent, creative, and generative. Our profession holds that the client is capable of finding their own answers and tapping into their own wisdom.[35]

As we discussed in the Principle of Uniqueness, relationship systems are living entities with their own lifetime arc. Companies and marriages are

---

35 **ICF** defines **coaching** as partnering with clients in a thought-provoking and creative process that inspires them to maximize their personal and professional potential.

born, they thrive, and they die. Each one has its own unique character, and like all living entities, each system has its own creativity and intelligence. Systems use this intelligence to be responsive to emergent events that happen to them. Like any living thing, they must adapt to survive. There's been a lot of talk about "organizational nimbleness," or the capacity of companies to keep up with the relentless evolution of the market. In the same way, families must cope with stressors like illness, divorce, new family members, and deaths. In many ways, the individual character of a relationship system is shaped in response to these external, emergent pressures.

In this chapter, we will look at the intelligence, creativity, and generativity inherent in relationship systems. We will also offer two Relationship Systems Intelligence approaches that powerfully support that development, Radical Responsibility, and the Designed Partnership Alliance.

RELATIONSHIP INTELLIGENCE

"So, relationship systems are intelligent and can find their own answers?" How many of us have thought, "Really? Not **this** system." When going through a divorce, or a business failure, it is hard to believe in the capacity of the system to figure things out. If your team is being laid off, trying to find the intelligence in the situation can feel like a fraud. In a bad patch of a marriage, we may be tempted to think that we are the only system in the world that is blind, stuck, and hopeless. Yet Relationship Warriorship is not about a flawless response, and **Right Relationship is not perfect relationship**. We are going to make mistakes. It is those mistakes that inform our intelligence and creativity. The key to relationship evolution is **recovery.** Learn from the mess and find a better way next time.

To get unstuck, we must be able to sit in the fire when it seems like everything is falling apart. We cannot be creative if there is no space for the new to emerge. At CRR Global, we sit in that fire with our certification students when we have "The Competency Talk." For most of us, the more we understand about relationships, the more we are aware of our own inadequacies. Relationship systems students often feel incompetent and that they are failures in their own relationships. I once had a student say to me, "If anyone knew about how bad I am at parenting, you would throw me out of the program." **All of us** sometimes feel like we suck at relationships. The road to mastering relationship systems intelligence involves four stages:

- **Unconscious incompetence**. This is blissful ignorance. We don't even know how much we don't know about relationships.

- **Conscious incompetence.** We are vividly aware of how much we don't know and how clumsy we are at relationships. This is an inevitable (and painful) stage of moving towards mastery.

- **Conscious competence.** We sometimes call this the training wheels stage. We are beginning to ride our relationship bike skillfully, but we still fall over a lot. We are working hard to improve, but our performance is spotty.

- **Unconscious competence.** This is the mastery level. At this stage, we are able to flow with circumstances in creative ways. We may not get it right the first time, but we learn from the feedback and recover. It feels like the system is collaborating with us, rather than us wrestling things into place. We support the system to find the ways in which it is creative, generative, and intelligent. We trust emergence to show us the way and creatively respond to it. Less effort is required; we connect with our awareness, and the right approach slips into our hands.

Relationships are hard. That is why they are sometimes called the difficult yoga.

Relationship Systems Intelligence doesn't always mean a happy ending, or a way out. Sometimes organizations complete their life cycle like a buggy whip factory in the automobile age. Some of us have been through the hell of a divorce, frightened for our children and devastated in our self-esteem. Certainly, we cannot find much intelligence in those situations, nor are we always open to finding it. I do not want to minimize the pain and suffering of those times.

> *"And if you gaze for long into an abyss,*
> *the abyss gazes also into you."*
>
> – NIETZSCHE

As we grow as individuals, Relationship Warriorship means being open to the emerging intelligence of the moment. It might be a painful moment when we realize **this marriage cannot be saved,** and the new road to separation opens up. Perhaps your company experiences market challenges and hovers on the edge of recovery or bankruptcy. Or it might be a moment when you see the strain on your teenager's face and just sit with her rather than confronting her. Relationship Systems Intelligence is the doorway to the Lion's Roar when we are open to it. However, much of the time, we have a fixed idea of what **should** happen. To access Relationship Systems Intelligence, we have to work with emergence and all the voices of the system. We must let go of our own locus of control and work with **what is** rather than what we want it to be. We ask ourselves again, "What is trying to happen here?"

Now let's look at the second word of this principle, "creative."

RELATIONSHIP CREATIVITY

"**Creative:** relating to or involving the imagination or original ideas, especially in the production of artistic work. Change unleashes people's creative energy."

– OXFORD LANGUAGES

In the principle of emergence, we discussed how the COVID pandemic has been a huge adaptative challenge to companies. It has forced rapid evolutionary change. As years of developmental shift were forced into months, only those able to adapt were able to survive. Responding creatively is easier when we can dance with the emergent to create the new.

Relationship systems are meaning-making machines. In your own work, how have circumstances provided you with the raw materials to make new meaning?

Name a personal and a business situation where challenging circumstances forced you to become creative.

RELATIONSHIP GENERATIVITY

"The fundamental purpose of relationship is to be generative."

– CRR GLOBAL

Generativity is a defining feature of relationship. Get two or more people together for more than a few minutes, and they will start generating something. Step into an elevator, and immediately people start to generate thoughts about where to stand, whether to greet someone, thoughts about the outfit someone is wearing. We can't help it! Relationship is responsive and generative within seconds. What we generate together can be almost anything! We can generate thoughts, ideas, emotions, projects, babies, meals, religions, wars . . . the list is endless! **The basic purpose of relationship is to exchange information, to generate something.** The natural generativity of relationship dances with the emergent to create the new. An economic crisis is an uncontrollable emergent event. Yet, when we enter into relationship with that crisis, it becomes a generative force for good or for ill.

Generativity is going to happen whether we like it or not. The big question is . . . **what** do we want to generate together? Can we be conscious and intentional about what we are creating? Are we stumbling around in the dark, making messes, and not understanding why? The emergent is often an event, an external locus of control. What we create out of that event is up to us. Personally, I still spend plenty of time generating unconscious, unskillful thoughts, feelings, and actions in my relationships. I accidentally end up in a fight with my spouse and wonder, "How did that happen?" I never meant to hurt my daughter's feelings, but "Oops, I did it again." On a really bad day, I will blame it on the other person, "She made me do it!" "If only she hadn't . . ." And, of course, generativity usually does involve another person's input. In the dance of relationship, we somehow co-create the situation. We **will** respond to events; **how** we respond is up to us on an individual and collective level. We would like to introduce a skill that helps Relationship Warriors to become more conscious and intentional about what we are generating.

Radical Responsibility is the first Relationship Systems Intelligence tool associated with being intelligent, creative, and generative. We first introduced the concept of Radical Responsibility as an attribute of Relationship Warriorship. It is such an important aspect of human evolution we wanted to develop it further as part of the principle of generativity.

RADICAL RESPONSIBILITY

"Radical Responsibility means radically embracing 100 percent responsibility and ownership of each and every circumstance you face, day in and day out in your life. This completely goes beyond blame. Radical Responsibility is a trans-blame model; it is stepping out of the blame and shame paradigm altogether. By understanding your part in creating a given situation, you can begin to choose how to create your future, and fully take ownership of that."

— FLEET MAULL, AIKIDO MASTER

If we look at the circumstances we face in our life, we can often see that we did have some role in creating, allowing, or setting ourselves up for these circumstances in one way or another. With that insight and information, we can then make different choices that are going to lead to different results.

Radical Responsibility may sound brutal. Many of us are exhausted from the responsibilities we already have. Are we really responsible for every relationship event that happens to us in our lives? The locus of control donut tells us **no.** We have no control over many societal relationship events that happen to us. I am not responsible for my mother's addiction, for the neighborhood flood, for an economic crash. But ultimately, I **am** responsible for my response to that event. As the quote above points out, Radical Responsibility moves the locus of control out of blame and into the zone of personal choice. I may not have created systemic oppression, but I am responsible for my personal response to it in my life.

Philosopher Martin Buber said that when we encounter something and deeply connect with it, we become responsible for it. Not in some co-dependent way, but because I naturally **care for** that which I **care about**. When I bring all of myself to you and invest in our exchange, both entities are transformed. This is true for something as ordinary as rescuing a spider. It is hard to imagine a spider as a teacher, but when I find a spider in my bathtub, that spider creates a choice for me. My dialogue of ME voices inside might say, "Ugh, a spider. It would be easier to just kill it. I certainly can't just leave it there. Do I really have the time to go get a glass and a piece of paper and rescue it? What if it bites me?"

Another voice inside says, "But it is another living creature, and it might live if I put it outside."

"Oh, all right, I'll rescue it."

To say that the spider and I were transformed by the interaction may be a bit much. But I learned something about myself, and it certainly was transformative for the spider who got to live! It may sound trite, but we generated an experience together.

Radical Responsibility takes work, which is why it is an attribute of Relationship Warriorship. Why should any of us go to the effort of practicing it? The only reason to try it is to grow as a person and as a species. Practicing Radical Responsibility is a powerful road to personal and collective evolution. "What is my part in what is happening in the world? What is the 2 percent truth[36] in that critical comment about me?" It is the path I take to go from being a victim to being a collaborator with the emergent.

Can it be taken too far? Yes. The locus of control donut shows me what I can control, what I can influence, and what is not in my control. Even in situations I cannot control, I am responsible for my emotional reaction to them. Given any situation, what am I choosing to generate in thoughts, feelings, and actions? **Who will I choose to be right now?**

Nothing undercuts our ego faster than facing our contribution to the situation. Every encounter allows us to learn about ourselves. If you want to grow as a person, look deeply into the part you play in any situation. Below are some examples of Radical Responsibility in the ME, YOU/ME, and WE systems. We also include some inquiries to open the process up to your own experience. You will know best what the best inquiries and actions will be for you personally.

---

36 This references the 2 percent truth exercise, which comes from the Path course of our training curriculum. This rule says that even if 98 percent of what someone says about us is incorrect, there is always 2 percent that is true about what they say. If we are willing to examine and own that 2 percent, we can integrate marginalized aspects of ourselves, increase our emotional range, and be less defensive! The easiest format is simply to say, "Well if only 2 percent of what they said about you was true, what would that be?" You can also ask, "How does this characteristic live in your relationship?"

RADICAL RESPONSIBILITY AND THE ME SYSTEM

To practice Radical Responsibility in the ME system, I have to be in relationship with all my inner sub-personalities. I need to be in communication with them and responsible for them. The best way to do that is through applying a set of powerful questions.

"I want to lose weight, and yet I ate the whole bag of chips. How did I generate all that chip eating?"

- What happened? What was I feeling? Did I make a conscious decision to eat them? Was I even present to eating them, or did I eat them on autopilot?

- Who in my ME system is the chip eater? What does that subpersonality look like? How old is he/she/they?

- What does the chip eater say about why they need to eat them?

- Let's have a dialogue with the chip eater. What does he/she/they have to say to me? A true relationship requires communication both ways.

- What am I feeling about what the chip eater says? Do I feel judgmental? Controlling? Understanding? What are the two of us generating in terms of emotions together right now?

- What does the chip eater say she/he/they need from ME to be in better relationship? Am I just trying to control that part, or am I open to a conversation with their voice of the system?

- Can I move to being creative with that side of me? Can I work out something that respects the chip eater's needs as well?

We have deliberately chosen a trivial event in the above situation. The encounter would be much more powerful if the ME topic were losing my temper, drinking too much, or ignoring the breast lump. Each internal dialogue has the power to generate more understanding of myself and, with that, change my behavior.

RADICAL RESPONSIBILITY AND THE YOU/ME SYSTEM

In the same way, Radical Responsibility to and with another person can be profound.

I have a fight with my son. He wants to put off going to medical school for a year so he can go backpacking around Europe. I think he is being irresponsible, and I worry he could lose his position at med school. He wants to have some fun before starting the med school slog. We trigger each other and generate considerable yelling, accusations, and frustration. We finish by storming out. Here are some steps our Third Entity might go through on the way to being intelligent, generative, and creative together.

- *We start out locked in our separate spaces. Both of us brood and generate justifications for why "**I am right, and they are wrong!**" After a while, we start to wear out the triggered feelings. Clearing out the emotional field within us is the first stage of recovery.*

- *After our anger individually cools, the feelings may shift to feeling sad or a little guilty and remorseful. This is not what either of us wants. What is trying to happen?*

- *My son, in an act of Radical Responsibility, reaches out to me in a repair attempt by suggesting we talk. I now have the choice to accept that repair attempt and generate a new opportunity to connect. Or I can refuse that olive branch and retreat back to step one of withdrawal and self-justification.*

- *I choose Radical Responsibility and consider: how can I shift my own position to a more creative one? To work with myself, I practice the Third Entity exercise, working on my own, with my own imagination. When I step into the ME position, I imagine telling my son all my concerns, what I feel, and what I want. When I step into experiencing my son's position, I can acknowledge that he just wants to have some freedom and adventures before he gets tied down in medical school. When I feel like I understand his position better, I am ready to step into the Third Entity position. This is the voice of our relationship itself. The Third Entity's voice reminds me that we love each other, and this is just one small rough life patch in a long life together. I remember that I want him to be happy as well as successful. I think about what I want to generate between us the next time we talk.*

- *When I have completed my exercise, I go back to my son. I apologize for losing my temper and tell him why I got triggered. I talk about what I learned in my internal Third Entity exercise and how I want to generate more mutual understanding in our next conversation. We have both practiced Radical Responsibility by considering our individual contribution to the conflict, and by striving to empathize with the other's needs. We are both wanting to move forward in a more constructive way.*

- *Now my son and I can apply the next Relationship Systems Intelligence tool that will help us be more creative together in the future. We practice creating a Designed Team Alliance (DTA) together before we pick the topic up again. The DTA helps us to generate a container and set of ground rules to help us have a constructive conversation. We will explore the Designed Team Alliance in greater depth in the next section.*

RADICAL RESPONSIBILITY AND THE WE

If CRR Global had a nickel for every time we were asked to address accountability issues with teams, we would be extremely wealthy. As we talked about in the Locus of Control section, organizations are often rife with blaming and finger-pointing. Teams with low locus of control are also likely to be low in task initiation and problem-solving, all of which affect accountability. Developing a culture of Radical Responsibility is challenging if people are only there for the paycheck. A sense of belonging and common purpose is a critical ground condition for creating an engaged workforce.

According to an Indeed survey, 46 percent of job seekers who considered a job but did not apply for it said they ultimately chose not to apply because they didn't feel it would be a good cultural fit. Culture matters. Several IBM Studies indicate that changing employee mindsets was one of the most difficult issues for CEOs.[37] The more input employees have in creating organizational culture, the more invested they are in maintaining it.

The Designed Team Alliance (DTA) is a simple and powerful tool for creating Radical Responsibility in relationship systems. Most of us have been accustomed to creating behavioral working agreements like "leave your cell phones on this desk," or "return emails within forty-eight hours." Working agreements are very useful in establishing behavioral norms. The DTA is something a little different. It is about harnessing the intelligence and creative capacity of the system and consciously generating a relationship culture together. Most companies know the importance of

---

[37] In a 2014 IBM report, "Making change work . . . while the work keeps changing: How Change Architects lead and manage organizational change," authors Hans-Henrik Jorgensen, Oliver Bruehl and Neele Franke found that "becoming a Change Architect constitutes a major organizational change itself—it requires leading a shift in mindset and behaviors of the whole organization."

developing a clear mission, vision, and values. In fact, according to a survey for Indeed.com, 72 percent of job seekers say it's extremely important to see details about company culture when applying for a job application. These cultural details generally include the mission, vision, and values for doing the work. The DTA is an extension of this process because it is about setting values and expectations for how to **be in relationship** with each other at work. Who do we want to be together? According to Gallup, the average person spends 81,396 hours working (and the only thing we do more than that is sleeping!). In its 2021 analysis of the World's workers, Gallup found that "60 percent of people are emotionally detached at work and 19 percent report being 'miserable.'" As the adage goes, employees don't quit bad jobs; they quit bad bosses.

We believe this is an evolutionary moment for business. We spend half our life at work. What if one of the important "products" of every company was employee satisfaction and happiness? Organizational culture can be consciously and intentionally generated. If we are going to spend that much time at work, let's find a way to enjoy it more.

The Designed Team Alliance helps us to recognize that we are responsible for creating the kind of culture we want to work in. Let's acknowledge that feelings are always in the building. There are secret love affairs, hostile gossip, rivalries, health crises, addictions, and home problems happening all the time. Let's stop pretending those feelings are not there and find a better way to work with them. The first step is acknowledging that we do have some control over the kind of culture we create.

We sometimes wish that it felt better at work or that we could improve our interactions with our family. The problem is we don't know how. The Designed Team Alliance is a tool that can be applied to any type of system just by changing a letter. There is the Designed Partnership Alliance (DPA) for YOU/ME systems; there are also Designed Coaching Alliances (DCA), Designed Family Alliances, etc. Any time we want to generate an agreed-upon culture and take responsibility for it, we can apply the Designed Team Alliance. Let's use an example of using the Designed Team Alliance to help a diverse group of stakeholders align. **The DTA can be run by anyone who is empowered by the group to facilitate it.**

A county health organization is creating an initiative to improve health access for diabetic adolescents. They are pulling together a variety of stakeholders, including the American Diabetes Association, local clinics, schools, pediatric hospitals, parents, and representatives from the diabetic adolescent community. All the different stakeholders come from very different perspectives and concerns. Before they can work effectively, the facilitators help them develop some working agreements to begin to forge an effective coalition. If they are going to work together, it helps to create conscious and intentional relationship. One of the tools they can use is the Designed Team Alliance (DTA). Below are the questions designed to help them develop an effective working culture. After each question is posed, the group discusses it together and records their agreements.

We start the Designed Team Alliance by providing a context for what and why we are doing the tool. It might go something like this:

"You represent a wide variety of agencies and groups with a common goal of improving healthcare for adolescent diabetics. You all have the same goal but come from very different perspectives. I'm going to introduce you to a tool that helps to create a certain culture or atmosphere and shared responsibility for your work together."

So, as you work together:

Question 1 – "What is the atmosphere you want to create in your working culture"?

In other words, how do you want it to feel when you are working together? This project is going to take some time. How do you want it to feel when you are interacting? After some discussion, the group might agree that the culture they want to generate includes:

- *Respect for each other*
- *Openness to different views*
- *Keeping a sense of humor*
- *Collaboration*

To make the agreements more concrete, the facilitators ask, "How would you know that respect is present?" (Or openness, etc.) A few people respond, "Taking each other seriously and really listening." "Practicing asking questions, not just advocating for one idea." "Respectful language."

Question 2 – "What would this working group need to really thrive together?" *This question really raises the bar for teams. Everyone wants a good working culture, but what does it mean to "thrive" as a team? The DTA helps us to make the invisible visible.*

*The first question (atmosphere) tends to tap into the basic requirements they want for a work culture. It evokes things like respect, collaboration, full participation, and accountability. The thrive question pushes the team into even more Radical Responsibility. What does it even mean to thrive as a team? This question often makes a team laugh a little bit. Someone shouts, "**Fun,**" and the facilitators follow up with, "What would fun look like for this group?" Someone says, "Getting together socially once in a while."*

*Other members do **not** want any more social commitments, so the group agrees to a social hour at the end of the week, just for those who choose* *to join in. Other suggestions for how to thrive include: "celebrating the successes, learning from each other." Again, the facilitators encourage them to get concrete about the kind of behaviors that would demonstrate that. They agree to begin meeting with other stakeholders, presenting a fifteen-minute talk on their particular perspective on adolescent diabetes. During one meeting, the diabetic teens might talk about their experience. At another meeting, it might be the pediatricians or parents. It is important to remember that every system will be unique in terms of what **thriving** means to them, depending on their age, their industry, etc. Introverts and extroverts may have very different ideas about what **fun** means. But the research is clear that cultures with high levels of positivity have lower rates of turnover and high levels of productivity.*[38]

Question 3 – "How do you want to be with each other when things get difficult?"

*This powerful question totally normalizes the fact that teams always **do** have difficult times. The question is, what kind of difficult times do **we** get into? When the inevitable happens, it is good to have a plan for what to do about it. It acknowledges that all systems have conflicts or failures, whatever "difficulties" means to them. Simply acknowledging that and normalizing it is often a big relief. "We are not 'screwed up,' all teams have troubles sometimes." The team now knows what to do when problems arise because they talked about how to handle it.*

This question helps the team to think about recovery when the agreements go wrong.

---

38 In the 2015 HBR article, "Proof That Positive Work Cultures Are More Productive," Seppälä and Cameron write: "Even when workplaces offered benefits such as flex time and work-from-home opportunities, engagement predicted wellbeing above and beyond anything else. Employees prefer workplace wellbeing to material benefits."

A common team discussion might be:

- *Person #1 – "If you have a problem with me, come to me directly, don't go to somebody else and complain about me."*

- *Person #2 – "Okay, but sometimes I need to process it with someone else before I know what I need to say."*

- *Person #1 – "I don't mind if you need to vet it with someone else first, but I want to know that you will come to me directly after that. I don't want to hear it from someone else."*

- *Person #3 – "Okay, so our written agreement is: if we find ourselves complaining about someone behind their back, we will take it back to that person directly within a day?"*

- *Team – "Agreed."*

Conflicts, broken agreements, and failures are information that the system needs to work with. The temptation is to finger-point, which shuts everyone down. Blaming is not compatible with psychological safety. Curiosity, and Radical Responsibility, however, open the situation up with questions like: "What happened?" "How do we not do that again?" "Okay, this was our part in the problem." Instead of "Who is doing what to whom, what is trying to happen here?"

Research suggests it is very helpful to discuss conflicts and create agreements in advance. In the book Great Business Teams, Howard Guttman outlines the key attributes of high-performing teams, one of which includes agreed-upon protocols for decision-making and conflict resolution.

Question 4 – "How do you want to handle it when someone breaks an agreement?"

One of the ways in which things get difficult is when someone breaks an agreement. This may happen on the YOU/ME level, or it may happen on the WE level. For example, the parents of diabetic kids may feel the pediatricians don't respect the initiative because they fail to show up reliably to the meetings. When working with broken agreements, it helps to figure out which systemic level should be addressed. YOU/ME conflicts are often best aired privately rather than exposing the whole team to the difficulty. But sometimes, they need to be addressed at the whole team level. The absence of pediatricians may reveal the need to create more flexible meeting times. Or it may reveal a professional privilege issue that is not being addressed. It is critically important to address breaches in the DTA and not to step over them. The DTA is only as effective as people's commitment to follow it.

- *"Well, if someone breaks an agreement, I would want to know why. There might be a good reason for it."*

- *"And what do we need to change so it doesn't get broken again? How can we learn from it?"*

The DTA is a living document that needs to be updated, reviewed, and corrected regularly in order to remain relevant. The Friday social meetings, which were part of the **fun** commitment, may lapse because the team is in a production crunch time. The new **fun** agreement may be to resume them once the production rush is over, or maybe to hold them only once a month. We recommend that teams review their DTA at least once a month. It's also important to update or revise it as new people enter the system.

The Designed Team Alliance provides a powerful tool to help systems develop Radical Responsibility. It supports teams to understand that they are the ones who create the culture of a team or organization. In teams with high command and control structures, the team members have less locus of control and, therefore, less initiative for co-creating a culture. If we want engaged employees, it is important for them to feel that their voice is important and impactful.[39]

39 Some industries require high command and control governance. This would include the military, the operating room, the police; any industry that needs immediate unequivocal command. One faculty member worked with a nuclear power plant team who pointed out that during an emergency, there was no time for designing an alliance about actions. The chain of command needed to be clear, and immediate compliance was critical. However, they also agreed the DTA was appropriate for routine operations and day-to-day policy.

THE DESIGNED TEAM ALLIANCE AND PRACTICING FAMILY VALUES

Of course, families are also naturally intelligent, creative, and generative. We encourage families and couples to discuss the principles they want to live by in their own system. Sometimes, these values are folded into religious beliefs. For example, "Do unto others as you would have them do unto you." But what does it mean to "do unto others as you would have them do unto you," when you are in a fight on the playground, or when a neighbor has a different political belief? The Designed Team Alliance together with the Thursday night seminars, helps us to operationalize our values intelligently. The tension between real-life pressures and trying to live our principles provides opportunities for amazing discussions, debates, and teachable moments. It is how we help ourselves and our children to reflect and to evolve.

Four decades ago, there was a lot more homophobia about gay relationships than there is now. At that time, my daughter Erin was four, and she came back from kindergarten in tears. A little girl had asked her about her mother, and she had said that she had two mommies. This led to a round of ridicule where she was told she couldn't have two mommies and that was **queer.**

This is the moment that every gay parent dreads. Erin was confused, and I wasn't going to wade into the complexities of sexuality and homophobia with a four-year-old. Yet, this was a reality that she was going to come up against in her life; how could I help her understand her family and society from a four-year-old's perspective? What could we generate out of this situation?

"Mom, why did she call you queer?"

"Queer means when two women love each other or when two men love each other."

"But why is it bad for two women to love each other?" (This question broke my heart.)

"In our family, we don't believe it is wrong to love someone, whether it is two women, a man and a woman, or two men. Loving someone is never a bad thing."

"But why did it make her mad?"

"Sometimes people get angry when there is something that they don't understand."

"I love you. Does that mean I am queer?"

"No, queer means when two women choose each other as life partners instead of choosing a husband."

"Well, she yelled that I was queer all over the yard! She was mean."

"I am so sorry that happened to you, sweetheart. You need to know that not everyone will understand if you say you have two mommies. Some will, and some won't. You and I know it is never a bad thing to love someone. And you get to decide who you trust to share that with and who you don't trust to share it with. Let's talk about how you want to handle it."

Erin went away to think about it, and later, she said, "I still don't understand why it is bad to love somebody. But I don't want to be called names. So, unless someone has two mommies too, I won't tell other people, or else it will be all over the playground."

Erin was designing an alliance with herself, her friends, and with me. This very real-life situation forced my daughter and me to confront a conflict between our family values of love is love, regardless of gender, and the fact that society would not always support that value. I was brokenhearted that at the age of four, she was already subjected to homophobia. I wanted to tell her to be loud and proud about having two mommies. But in 1978, we were still decades away from legal gay marriage, and discrimination was a very real thing. It was a teachable moment where my daughter grasped two truths: love has no boundaries, and discretion is sometimes the better part of valor.

What is it that you would like to generate around family values with your own children? Do your values sometimes conflict with other peoples'? What alliances might you need to design around those conflicts?

DESIGNED TEAM ALLIANCES ARE IMPORTANT

The Designed Team Alliance is about Radical Responsibility because it stands for, "We are choosing together the feelings and actions needed for the kind of relationship we want." In the process, we develop EQ, "What do **I** actually want?" SI, "What do **you** want?" and RSI, "What kind of a culture do **we** want to create together?" Designed Team Alliances are aspirational. They are about planning for the kind of partnership we hope for. Do they always work? No! Relationships are always a work in progress. However, the Designed Team Alliance gives us the chance to design how we want to negotiate together when things (inevitably) do go off course.

A company climate is not just a set of behaviors; it is a **feeling**. The idea that a team can influence how their workplace feels is sometimes shocking to teams. We have heard things like, "What do feelings have to do with the work?" One team suggested that it was not their place to co-design the culture of the company. It was the owner's company, and **he** should decide the values and atmosphere. There is sometimes a vague terror that if emotions are openly invited, the teams will devolve into a weeping, raging morass. But morale and company climate research have repeatedly shown **how it feels to be at work** is a critical component of employee retention and satisfaction.[40]

The Designed Team Alliance is a living document and should be reviewed and revamped as circumstances change. It is a training tool to help teams and families access their creativity and intelligence by getting clear about what they want, what success would look like, and what to do when they fail. That is a lot of Radical Responsibility! Do companies ever achieve that thriving culture? Yes, often for long periods of time. However, the DTA is an aspiration, what we want to strive for together! We may never fully get there.

Also, what we want for our culture will inevitably change. A team may start with a generic term like respect, but over time they realize that what they actually want is acknowledgment. Change up the questions as needed by circumstances. Just the process of reviewing the DTA helps the team to mature in their EQ, SI, and RSI. One secret about the Designed Team Alliance: while the written agreement is important, it is less important than the process of getting there! It is the talking together, the exploration, and the co-creation that helps teams become intelligent, creative, and generative.

---

40 In the 2008 IBM Study, "Making Change Work," eight out of ten CEOs anticipated substantial or very substantial change over the next three years, yet they rated their ability to manage change as 22 percent lower than their expected need for it. The main obstacles they identified were changing mindsets and attitudes (58 percent) and corporate culture (49 percent).

SOME CLOSING WORDS ON RADICAL RESPONSIBILITY

It takes a healthy ego to be strong enough to take responsibility. And like all strong medicine, we need to titrate our level of exposure to it. Taking Radical Responsibility for everything, all the time would be withering and co-dependent. But even if only as an exercise, it is a profound way of building the muscle of Relationship Warriorship. We have a generative role in the events of our families, businesses, and lives. The more responsibility we take, the stronger our agency in the world. Here are a few tips that can make the journey easier:

- Be gentle with yourself. **Radical Responsibility is a practice, not an outcome.** When we are building a new muscle, we don't start by lifting the heaviest weight. Start with something that feels manageable.

- Look deeper. **Why** do you want to practice Radical Responsibility? What is in it for you, or for the rest of the system that will keep you motivated? Ask your family and teams what they think about practicing Radical Responsibility.

- Radical Responsibility can happen on the level of action, mind, or emotions. I may change how I behave with someone, learn about a new approach, or simply explore my feelings. This takes time. I may start with the awareness that certain things trigger me emotionally. I might then explore my ME system to better understand those feelings. Finally, I might plan and execute a new way of dealing with the situation. As they ask in middle school, do I want to be helped, heard, or hugged? Radical Responsibility is a form of empowerment since it increases my sense of what I can influence or control.

- Be gentle with yourself (again)! There are some situations where I can practice Radical Responsibility and some places where my Radical Responsibility muscle is just not strong enough. Sometimes, it feels easier to blame someone else. We will fail over and over again. The point is **to recover.**

"I walk down the street.
There is a deep hole in the sidewalk.
I fall in.
I am lost . . . I am helpless.
It isn't my fault.
It takes forever to find a way out.

I walk down the same street.
There is a deep hole in the sidewalk.
I pretend I don't see it.
I fall in again.
I can't believe I am in the same place.
But, it isn't my fault.
It still takes me a long time to get out.

I walk down the same street.
There is a deep hole in the sidewalk.
I see it is there.
I still fall in. It's a habit.
My eyes are open.
I know where I am.
It is my fault. I get out immediately.

I walk down the same street.
There is a deep hole in the sidewalk.
I walk around it.

I walk down another street."

— PORTIA NELSON, "THERE'S A HOLE IN MY SIDEWALK:
THE ROMANCE OF SELF-DISCOVERY"

CHAPTER 16

PRINCIPLE – SYSTEMS RELY ON ROLES FOR THEIR ORGANIZATION AND EXECUTION OF FUNCTIONS

SYSTEMS RELY ON ROLES FOR THEIR ORGANIZATION AND EXECUTION OF FUNCTION

Let's quickly review our progress through the principles.

Principle – Every relationship system is unique. This gives us the character of the system—its particular personality.

Principle – Emergence is natural to all relationship systems, introducing change and shaping that system. Every relationship system has to improvise with changing circumstances.

Principle – Every member of a system is the voice of that system. Each voice of the system provides a critical contribution to the chorus of the Third Entity.

Principle – Systems are naturally creative, intelligent, and generative. Like a jazz ensemble, the Third Entity weaves the different experiences of the system to create something new.

Principle – Systems rely on roles for the organization and execution of their functions. Roles are the critical templates that systems pick up or put down when they need to accomplish something.

"A role is a function with a certain set of responsibilities."

– CRR GLOBAL

A role may be temporary and straightforward, like grocery shopper, or it may be long-term and complex, like parent. Roles are how systems get things done. Each role is a short job description of what to do that acts like a template or map. So, if a group of strangers comes together for a friendly game of baseball, everybody knows what the pitcher needs to do. The actions of each player are encoded in their role. So, roles are **efficient.** Systems are often large and interdependent; roles help to organize who does what and when.

Let's say a group of game visionaries have a great idea for building a new gaming company. They're brilliant as game designers, but they know nothing about running a business. They recognize they need a ton of other employee roles to be successful. They need investors, someone to handle the technical requirements, an R&D department . . . the list goes on! Every start-up knows this. Each role has encoded tasks and behaviors that the other roles depend on.

GEM

If you remember back to the Basics, we discussed how no individual is a single entity. Instead, we are more like a cut gemstone. We are one single, beautiful gem of a person, but we have multiple functions. As we navigate our day, different roles will pop up—perhaps the side of me that's a supervisor or my role as a golfer. All these dozens of roles make up the fullness of the ME system. So, every person is an integrated self (the gemstone we think of as ME), but we have multiple facets of self, or roles, that make us flexible and give us range. This is true for every type of system. Roles are so familiar to us that we take them for granted. We unconsciously navigate our day, moving from role to role.

I wake up in the morning, and after coffee, I wrangle the kids out of bed (parent role) and drop them off at school (chauffeur role). At work, I put on my security badge, which slides me into a professional role. I have a lunch date with a close co-worker, and I'm in my friend role. I grab a quick game of racket ball (player role) before I head home to cook dinner (cook role) before putting the kids to bed (parent) and relaxing with my spouse (partner role).

For pairs, the moment we meet somebody new, we start figuring out our roles, so we know how to behave together. I will cook, and you wash the dishes. In the WE system, if we're going on a group trip, we might want to assign one person to check out the hotels, another to book the tickets, and someone else to organize a babysitter. Often, we don't even think about it; we just adopt a role that needs doing. It is second nature to us.

The problem with roles is that they can become rigid. It is like coloring inside a set of lines. Yet, my template of what it means to be a wife, or a CEO may be very different from your template. Whose template are we using? Conflicts are generated when we have different assumptions of what a particular role should entail. Roles are multi-layered, with several different categories.

OUTER ROLES

OUTER ROLES

Outer roles are all about job function: how to do the things we do. These roles are deeply familiar to us; they tell us how to behave. What's interesting is **that outer roles are determined by the needs of the system.** The unique character of the system demands that certain roles be occupied. For example, a company needs a CEO to function. CEO is an outer role, a job function. CEOs come and go, and different people with different styles may occupy that role. But, the fact that the CEO role even exists is dictated by the needs of the company. A family system needs a bread-winner, a cook, a bill payer, etc. If we divorce our wife Maria and remarry Esther, the people change, but the outer role of spouse remains. The role is just occupied by someone else. So, while we might divorce someone or fire an employee, the roles themselves persist and can be occupied by the next person. Again, tension will arise in a relationship when my particular template for an outer role is different from yours. Esther may be a very different style of spouse than Maria.

When I was a psychology intern, I juggled the roles of mother and wife with my work. I typically left the office around five to get home because I also had responsibilities as a mom and a spouse. At the time, I was supervised by a psychologist who was single and had no children. She felt it was unprofessional for me to leave work at closing time. Why didn't I stay late to finish extra work, or even start tomorrow's work? From her perspective, a good intern stayed late and worked many hours. In fact, there wasn't a boundary around how many hours you worked. You just did whatever it took. But my supervisor's intern role template didn't work with my life, with my small child, my marriage, and my carpool. So, we ended up having a fight about my leaving work at five. To her credit, she was able to own that her template for the intern role was shaped by her own training experience when she was much younger and single. When she was an intern, her whole life was work.

So, she put in ten to twelve hours a day working and just assumed that this was the role template for being an intern. However, my intern role template said something different: "Well, wait a minute. I've signed a contract for a certain number of hours, and while I am happy to put in extra time at home, I need to be home at a certain time so that I can pick up my baby and be available for my family." **My** *contract about what it meant to be an intern enabled me to honor my other roles as wife and mother. Thankfully, my boss and I were able to talk about this, and we agreed that her particular intern template didn't work in my life. I was older, and I had more role complexities in my personal life. We were able to work it out.*

Role negotiation is constantly happening in every relationship. Being an intern also meant that I had to adjust my roles at home in order to meet my professional responsibilities. Systems are constantly working to meet and align the complexities of outer roles. Let's make some of these role conflicts more visible.

RELATIONSHIP WARRIORSHIP EXERCISE

- List some of the outer roles (teacher, father, husband) that you have in your life.

- How do these roles compete or conflict (for example, work roles place a strain on your marriage)?

- If you are having strains between roles, what kind of Designed Team Alliances do you need to co-create to address some of those strains?

Outer roles give us templates to know how to behave in a given job function. Using the Designed Team Alliance can help us to co-create agreements about what that job template looks like.

INNER ROLES

Inner roles help to regulate **the emotional functioning of a relationship.** So, while outer roles tell us how to behave, inner roles regulate the emotional "housekeeping" of the system.

Under the surface of any relationship, there are a host of emotional events occurring that are rarely talked about. Just like outer roles, inner roles are also dictated by the character of the Third Entity, the system itself. Every team/family will have certain basic emotional needs. For example, someone needs to bring up difficult things that need to be talked about (disturber). This is often paired with a role that smooths things over (peacemaker). A sunny optimistic role may cheer the team up, while the vigilant role watches for threats. Teams often have a party person who knows when we need to celebrate. The inner role list goes on. Every unique relationship has its own emotional needs. Any member in the system can pick up and play different emotional role depending on the needs of that system.

So, how do we know that inner roles are being dictated by the system? Well, we don't always like certain roles even though they're needed. For example, we may fire a disturber because they are disruptive, like the beach master.[41] Yet, as the beach master demonstrates, disturbers are a useful role for the system. Disturbers are the ones that point out problems, challenge assumptions, and demand that we address difficult issues. It is **the style** of how a role is occupied that determines whether it is a constructive role or not. The beach master held the disturber role with a toxic style. A different person could probably occupy that role with a lot more

41 Our controller at CRR Global has an imaginary contract clause called the PITA clause. She told me it was the *"Pain in the Ass"* clause! This is not a real contractual clause, obviously, but it does encourage us to consider how much trouble a disruptive client is worth. And do we need to charge more for that?

emotional intelligence and skillfulness. So, if we fire one of these roles, like disturber, what happens? Well, generally, if we lose an employee that plays an important emotional role, someone else will pick up that role because the system will demand it. Inner roles often come in pairs to balance each other out. A disturber needs a peacemaker. The compassionate role requires balance through an accountability role. The character of the family members will partly dictate what inner roles we take on. For example, you may be the pursuer in one relationship and find yourself the distancer in another. Or maybe you were the strict parent in one marriage and find yourself the lenient parent in the next. If one partner is stronger at one inner role, then the other may navigate to the opposite role to balance the polarity. The distribution of emotional styles in a team or a family reflects the different needs of that unique Third Entity.

This is particularly true with couples. Couples often unconsciously work out what psychological roles they will play, particularly in important areas like conflict. Some couples are highly expressive in conflicts; they are comfortable yelling at each other or making dramatic gestures. For them, conflict comes up like a storm and then blows out to sea. But other couples may find that expressive style too provocative. They become at risk of escalating into increasing anger rather than moving toward resolution. In healthy couples, often one member of the pair will pick up the role of de-escalating the quarrel, lowering the volume, and making more repair bids. They are not abandoning their position; they are instinctively lowering the temperature of the conflict. They are bringing more awareness and caution to the situation.

OUTER AND INNER ROLE DIFFICULTIES

The great thing about outer and inner roles is that the system will let you know when there is difficulty. Both personal and work systems will signal to you when role problems arise. These difficulties can take different forms.

Role nausea. We have all had the experience of getting totally sick of holding a particular role. Maybe you are done with being the person who always brings up the problem. Perhaps you are not technically the IT person, but somehow, you are the one everyone goes to for minor computer problems. We experience role nausea when the cost of holding a particular inner or outer role has gotten too high. It is easy for a role to become conflated with the person. Because Neville usually cooks dinner, the family panics when he wants to take an evening class during dinner time. Neville = cook. When a role becomes our identity, we develop role nausea rapidly. It is easy to forget that a role is like a piece of clothing that we put on for the sake of the system. It does not define who we are. **You are not your role; you temporarily play a role for convenience**. When a person conflates their role with their identity, we can develop an identity crisis when that role is taken away. We see this in some retirees who struggle to find a purpose when they leave the workforce.

Role confusion. Of course, all roles shift with emerging circumstances. As a start-up becomes more successful, new roles will be needed, like an HR director or a company attorney. One signal that roles need to be redefined is role confusion. We often do an exercise with teams that looks at how many people have their hand in a particular task, for example, producing the company newsletter. The more people who are involved, the less efficient the role. In start-ups, roles are often assigned ad hoc, and role descriptions are sketchy. Role confusion creates a leak of resources, energy, and time.

Poorly occupied roles. We all have painful experiences with poorly occupied roles. If a role is like footwear, then a poorly occupied role is like wearing shoes two sizes too tight! Perhaps we are a visionary who somehow ends up responsible for administrative details. The person who is bad at math gets stuck with the monthly budget. People stuck in poorly occupied roles mean well but are simply not equipped to do the job. The role just doesn't fit them.

GHOST ROLES

A ghost role is something that cannot be seen but haunts a relationship system. It is often invisible until it is revealed, yet it impacts the relationship. Ghosts can be a person, living or dead, like feeling haunted by the ghost of your critical mother. They can also be a situation or event in the past or future, like the ghost of previous layoffs in a company.

Relationship ghosts are a fact of life, and they are everywhere. We all have them because survival requires us to remember the bad things that happened to us. When our human ancestors lived on the savanna, their brains needed to remember where they last saw a tiger. The brain then recognizes similar places where we might see a tiger as a survival mechanism. In today's world, the brain cannot tell the difference between a fright due to a real tiger or a fright due to a dressing down by our boss. The brain is designed to remember and remind us of potentially threatening situations.

Ghosts are an influence left in our relationship due to some kind of experience. The ghost of a jealous boyfriend will make us hypersensitive to signals of jealousy from the next boyfriend. Significant events can also create ghosts. I was involved in a serious car accident a few years ago, and whenever we drive past that spot on the road, Marita and I have a strong emotional memory of that time.

All of us are walking around wearing ghost glasses, which are coloring our experience of the world. One of the easiest ways to work with ghosts is to simply become aware of them. We can work with something once we are aware of it. Over time, we can learn to sense a ghost; it's like a subtle smell in the air. When something feels off or isn't adding up, then a ghost may be impacting that system. Below is a partial list of the kinds of ghosts that may be impacting your world. The memory of these events leaves a scar of some kind.

PERSONAL RELATIONSHIP GHOSTS

- Ex-intimate partners (spouses, boyfriends, girlfriends)
- Traumatic events (loss of a child, bankruptcy, death, divorce)
- History of addictions
- Severe illness, accidents, or family history of illness
- Relationship betrayals (affairs, fraud, separations)
- Experiences of discrimination like racism or gender bias

Any big events will leave a mark on personal relationships that may need to be addressed. However, many smaller events leave mini ghosts. Most of us have certain topics in our marriages that we try and avoid because there is a history of that topic being explosive. Perhaps we avoid talking about your mother because we always fight about her. Perhaps we can't talk about money, sex, or the kids because our amygdala knows, **"There be tigers there."** In a high-conflict marriage, it can start to feel like we are living in a field of land mines.

JACK AND SALLY

Jack and Sally have been married for nine years. Three years ago, Sally had a brief affair with a colleague when she was away on a business trip. The couple went to coaching and worked hard on the grief, pain, anger, and distrust this caused the relationship. They also worked on improving their relationship, so the marriage was more satisfying for both of them. Their marriage is stable now, except when Sally must go away on a business trip. When she is away, the ghost of the affair comes back up. Jack gets suspicious, insecure, and calls her ten times a day.

Sally: *"I am a senior manager. Travel comes with the job. You know that."*

Jack: *"Well, it makes me uncomfortable. After what happened three years ago, I spend my whole time wondering what's going on."*

Sally: *"I thought we worked all that through. I have apologized dozens of times for hurting you! I truly regret it, and I will never do that to you again. I am so sad I hurt this relationship. I know it takes time to build trust again, but we have to move past this."*

GHOSTBUSTING

Families and companies instinctively understand ghosts. ORSC is about making the invisible visible, and there is often a sense of relief when ghosts are finally named. Here are some basic steps for working with ghosts. It is easiest to have a third party to facilitate since ghosts can be triggering.

First, raise everyone's awareness about ghosts, so they can understand them. Education might sound like:

Facilitator: *"When something difficult has happened in a relationship, it leaves a ghost. A ghost is something that is not physically there but is haunting the relationship. Ghosts happen in every kind of relationship and type of business. It is a natural part of relationship."*

Next, name the ghost and explore the circumstances that created it. Since Sally's affair happened on a business trip, it makes sense that the ghost would come up for the couple when she travels now. Normalizing ghosts helps a system know that they are not crazy to have a reaction.

Facilitator: *"Given Sally's affair a few years ago, it's natural that this ghost would arise when she goes away again."*

Normalizing ghosts helps the system to relax and go on to the next step.

For the next step, explore the impact of the ghost on the relationship now. Take your time when unfolding the impact. It takes time to explore all the feelings.

Let's track these steps through Jack and Sally as they might have done with a facilitator:

Facilitator: *"How is the ghost of the affair impacting your relationship now?"*

Sally: *"Look, I know I really hurt you, but I have worked hard on rebuilding our connection. And that was three years ago! Isn't there a statute of limitations on this? You can't call me ten times a day, every day I'm away. I feel like you never trust me, and I can't get any work done."*

Jack: *"You broke my trust. Now, when you're away, I feel like I can't relax. I call because I'm anxious."*

The next step is to help the couple change their relationship with the ghost. The facilitator can do this by taking a simple object to represent the ghost, putting it between the couple, and having each of them hold one side of it so they are holding it together.

Facilitator: *"Jack and Sally, this object you are holding represents the ghost of the affair. Both of you are holding on to it. It is between the two of you and keeping you apart. The fights, the distrust, and the phone calls are all because of this ghost between you. What does it feel like having this thing always between you?"*

Sally: *"It sucks! I feel like everything blows up when I go away. And I miss feeling close to Jack. I've gotten to dread business trips."*

Jack: "Well, I hate it too. It is a horrible feeling."

Once the couple has taken some time to explore the impact of the ghost, Jack and Sally can physically move the object representing the ghost out from between them.

Facilitator: "Let's try something different. Together, put the ghost down somewhere so it's not between the two of you anymore. Put it out in front of you so you can see it."

*Jack and Sally put the object representing the ghost of the affair on the floor in front of them. Next, they can explore what it is like **not** to have the ghost between them.*

Facilitator: "Okay, so now the ghost of the affair is no longer stuck between you, and it's out there in front where you can both see it. Let's talk about what it would be like to **not** have this thing between you anymore."

Jack: "Well, it would be nice not to worry when you are gone. Maybe I could let go a little. It could feel good, like we are working on this together."

Sally: "I could feel like you trusted me. I don't want you to feel worried! It would be great to move past this thing together."

Now, the couple can return to a familiar tool, creating a Designed Partnership Alliance for how to work together on the ghost.

Facilitator: "Now that you have some idea of what it would be like to recover from this ghost, let's create a Designed Partnership Alliance about how to deal with the ghost in a better way. What is the kind of atmosphere you want to create together when Sally is away?"

Sally: "Trust!"

Facilitator: "How would you know you were trusted?"

Sally: "Jack wouldn't call me twelve times a day. We wouldn't fight every time I need to travel."

Jack: "Well, I need to feel safe."

Sally: "What would help you feel safe?"

Jack: "I need you to call me every night and not act like I am crazy. I want an atmosphere of connection and patience. I want you to understand that it is going to take me some time to develop trust, and I want you to be patient."

*Sally: "I **do** understand that it takes time, and I am happy to call you once a night. I get it, that you worry, and I want to support you. I just need you to make the effort to develop that trust too."*

Think ahead. Part of working with ghosts involves planning for what to do when the ghost rears its head again. Ghosts are sticky; part of their nature is that they are prone to coming back. Let's follow Jack and Sally through planning ahead.

Facilitator: "So, we know ghosts have a tendency to reoccur. How do you want to handle it when it crops up again?"

Jack: "Well, if you're late calling, I am going to start worrying again."

Sally: "I promise if I am going to call late or something unexpected happens, I will call or text you."

Finally, celebrate the successes in working with the ghost, not the failures. Ghostbusting takes time.

Facilitator: "So, let's talk about how this last business trip went."

Sally: "You still called me a lot."

Facilitator: "Okay, but can we talk about what you both did, right? What do you appreciate about how it went."

Sally: "Well, I appreciate that you called me a lot less than the last time. Also, we could talk about the ghost rather than fighting about it."

Jack: "I appreciate that you didn't get mad at me when I called. I felt like you understood I was just anxious, which helped me settle down."

Because ghosts are fear-based, it takes time for the brain to release and relearn how to let go. It is a good idea to set modest goals to increase the trust with each event. Small gains are good.

Sally: So, I'm going away in a few weeks. Let's set some new goals for developing trust together. How about we agree to talk **once** every day?"

Jack: "Okay, but I need a little more than that. How about you text me when you are leaving to go out, and we can talk when you get back."

Sally: "Deal."

ORGANIZATIONAL GHOSTS

Of course, organizations are also littered with the ghosts of difficult events. Situations that engender ghosts in companies are things like:

Personnel changes, especially if the person who left had a powerful positive or negative impact on the team. We once worked with a team where the previous manager, Gunther, had an unmanaged bipolar illness that eventually resulted in his leaving the company. It took many sessions for the team to work through the ghost of Gunther. They needed to understand their own reactions to his instability. They explored their confusion about his erratic behavior and talked about their feelings of helplessness around supporting their colleague. Much loved individuals also leave a ghost when they leave. The new manager may be resented just because they aren't the same person as the manager who left. It is hard for the new manager to live up to the ghost of the old one unless it can be named and discussed.

Traumatic emotional events like team deaths, reorganizations, lay-offs, and legal or criminal suits. When we worked with an organization forced to severely downsize, we worked with the ghost of "those who lost their jobs." The remaining team members needed to talk about their grief about their friends and guilt about being the survivors. There was an additional ghost around fear of another set of layoffs.

The ghost of "the way things used to be." Many employees struggle with the speed of change these days. When large organizational changes happen, like mergers, acquisitions, and restructures, there is always the ghost of "the good old days" or "the way things used to be." This is a natural stage of adjusting to change, and it can be accelerated by naming the old days as a ghost.

When your company is going through big shifts, it can be very helpful to walk through the steps of working with ghosts. In our experience, teams instinctively understand the concept of ghosts and are relieved to have them named.

 ## CLEARING OUT ORGANIZATIONAL GHOSTS

A county health organization was putting together a task force to improve healthcare coordination across three cities. The problem was that the cities had a history of conflict with county governments and with competing against each other for resources. The task force included representatives

from each city and the county health department. Everyone gave lip service to collaboration, but during the first meeting, the atmosphere was thick with old ghosts. Everyone in the task force had memories of failed attempts to work together or who had done what to whom. There was widespread distrust of the county health care administration. Finally, we did a ghostbusting exercise, including the following steps.

- *We had everyone write down two ghosts from the past on separate sticky notes. They were to pick the ghosts that were most interfering with developing a collaborative relationship now.*

- *We put the ghost sticky notes on a flip chart and ordered them by type. Often the same ghosts were mentioned by several people. There were:*

  - *Ghosts around a controlling county supervisor.*
  - *Ghosts around racial inequities when competing for county and state resources.*
  - *Ghosts around failed attempts at collaboration. "We spent hours on this, and nothing changed."*
  - *Ghosts around control and decision-making struggles.*

- *Each ghost was discussed using the following questions:*

  - *What is the story about this ghost (what happened)?*
  - *What was the impact of that event?*
  - *How is that ghost still haunting us today?*
  - *What did we learn from that ghost?*
  - *What do we need to move on from it?*
  - *What are our working agreements around it?*
  - *How will we be/do together if the ghost comes back?*

Again, where there are relationships, there will be ghosts! Because every system is unique, every company will have its own unique ghost profile.

SECRET SELVES (OR SUBPERSONALITIES)

So, outer roles give us WHAT we do (the job function). Inner roles give us the HOW we do it (the style of our emotional functioning). Finally, subpersonalities give us the WHO within us who will do any particular task.[42]

We are one entity, like the gemstone, but there are many subpersonalities within us. So, while we have the integrity of being "ME," different facets of our personality may emerge, featuring different qualities of who we are. If we don't have much EQ or awareness of our different subpersonalities, frankly, we can sometimes sound crazy! It sounds like we are constantly changing our minds as different selves rotate, though, with different opinions on the topic. *"Do subpersonalities mean that we are all Multiple Personalities?"* No, and yes. Most of us do not have the clinical diagnosis of dissociative disorder. Usually, the boundaries between our subpersonalities are permeable, and we can move between them fluidly and consciously. All of us have many, many aspects of self that we can access. Learning to work with our different selves is one of the fast roads to evolving as a person.

Roles and subpersonalities often overlap. Subpersonalities are different from outer and inner roles because they arise from our own personal psychology. Outer and inner roles are more like the props we can pick up or put down. Any subpersonality can also put on a role, like a piece of clothing. "The comedian" can be a temporary outer role, or it can become a more permanent aspect of self. Different subpersonalities will inhabit roles differently, as we learned from the beach master. The role of disturber is important to the system. But, some subpersonalities can be skillful in that role, and others may be too aggressive. Subpersonalities also differ from roles because, while inner and outer roles are determined

---

42 The concept of subpersonalities has many names and has been around for thousands of years. For example, in the ORSC courses, they are called Secret Selves.

by the needs of the system, **subpersonalities emerge from the individual self** (the ME system). They're developed by my personal history of proclivities, experiences, and relationships.

Some of these innate selves are great gifts, like the champion, the empath, or the protector. Others enter our personal mandala because of a painful experience: the abused child, the failure. Subpersonalities may feel similar to ghosts because they hang around our ME system. Group ghosts are shared and atmospheric, like a bad smell in the room. Subpersonalities are a part of the individual, a more active and powerful dynamic. Our many positive and triggered selves are constantly mediating our experience of life. Much of our mental health depends upon the relationships between these different facets of our selves. If I struggle with different aspects of myself, I may seek coaching or therapy to work with them.

There is a fascinating interplay between roles and subpersonalities. Do subpersonalities gravitate towards certain roles, or do roles slowly create subpersonalities? When we are way over an edge and unsure of how to act, we often rely on roles to give us a template for how to behave. If we are not sure how to be a "leader," we look for examples of how leaders "should" behave. We try on and reject different styles of leadership, and slowly, over time, the role can evolve into our own authentic leader subpersonality. A young mother looks to the role models around her as she forms her own personal subpersonality of parent. In this sense, both outer and inner roles provide me with templates as I evolve my own cast of subpersonalities. On the other hand, certain subpersonalities will naturally gravitate toward certain roles. If I have a strong healer subpersonality inside me, I will be attracted to outer roles like doctor or medic.

Alternatively, when we live an outer role long enough, it becomes part of our identity. This can create an identity crisis when a role is taken away from us. Surgeon is not just an outer role; it becomes an important aspect of who I am. When it's time to retire, I may have a crisis of character. Who am I if I am not a surgeon anymore? I once worked with a mother whose only child died. Part of her pain was wondering, "If I do not have a child, am I still a mother?" In this way, roles and subpersonalities shape and influence one another. In a way, we have to act it to become it. Outer and inner roles act as training wheels until we can integrate a new aspect of self. Our identity is fluid and in constant evolution. Roles and subpersonalities help us develop range and flexibility.

Manuel is a successful doctor with a large and complex practice. He enjoys his work but is also feeling burned out and exhausted. Like everyone else, Manuel is a gemstone with many subpersonality facets. Let's explore a few of them.

- *__The clinician__ – Both an outer role and a subpersonality, the clinician loves his job and works hard. He is ambitious and enjoys a challenge. This self also feels pressure to support his medical practice by working more hours than he can sustain. He is a perfectionist and feels guilty about taking time off.*

- *__The take-it-easy self__ – This subpersonality feels exhausted and lazy and just wants to slow down and go at a more human pace. This self sleeps through the alarm and wants to chat with the kids until he is hopelessly late for work. He also just can't seem to get to meetings on time or finish his paperwork. This pattern, of course, drives the clinician crazy.*

- *__The artist__ – This subpersonality is constantly frustrated that he doesn't have time to be creative. This self is a sculptor who likes to contribute his pieces to local art shows. He hasn't made it to his studio in years and feels crowded out by the clinician and take-it-easy. He complains that those selves are always working or recovering from working. There* *is just not enough time and energy left to be creative. This self feels "there must be more to life."*

Every single one of these subpersonalities plays an important part in making Manuel the person that he is. And clearly, these selves have different agendas and values. Part of Manuel's burnout comes from the lack of balance and full expression of all of who he is. In addition, these selves are fighting with each other. Take it easy sabotages the clinician. The clinician won't let take it easy take a vacation. The artist gets no voice at all but makes his feelings known by depressing the whole system. Every one of these selves is a critical part of Manuel's ME system. There is just not time for all of them.

We believe that many of the ills of society: the lack of engagement, illness, depression, and addiction, are due to the inability to express the complexity of who we are. **Burnout is not just about too many hours of work; it is also about a loss of heart and meaning.** We are complex, multifaceted people often forced into rigid roles.[43] Are you a mother and a professional woman? Then you know the strain between those different roles and subpersonalities. Do you never see your kids or your spouse because you are running for political office? Are you a priest who is also in a crisis of faith? We are all living with competing subpersonalities within us. These selves are our richness and our wealth, but there is hell to pay if we try to stifle any of them.

We all experience identity tensions every day of our lives. What is useful about the ORSC approach is that by reifying these selves, we can separate and hold them as **one part of who we are, not all of who we are.** No one subpersonality of who we are defines us. We are a whole complex system.

Jorge is a thirty-year-old father who has worked as a dental assistant for eight years and considers himself a family man. He loves his wife and his two boys, aged six and two. In his late teens, he struggled with heroin addiction and finally went into a rehab program and got clean. Then, a year ago, he injured his back in a skiing accident and ended up addicted to opioids. He returned to an addiction treatment program and is now working hard to stay clean. His relapse into addiction has left him with a primary identity of being **the addict.** *He believes that his relapse defines who he is as a person, and he has no confidence in his ability to recover. He believes, "I have always been an addict, and I will always be an addict."*

He is partially right. He has an addict subpersonality who will always be with him. For Jorge to recover, he must keep the addict as his primary focus for now. Without dealing with his addiction, nothing else can happen. He

---

43 If you've not seen it already, we'd highly recommend the Disney film *Inside Out*, which follows the inner workings inside the mind of a young girl named Riley. Five personified emotions administer her thoughts and actions as she adapts to her family's relocation.

and his family spend time working with Narcotics Anonymous and family therapy, discussing how to manage the impact of his addiction. He is now clean and sober, but after a year of intensive work, Jorge begins to feel that the addict has taken over everything. Was being an addict the summation of his life? Can he ever get back to the other parts of himself?

Jorge begins to work with the rest of his ME system. Yes, he has an addict inside, but he also has a father, a husband, a dental professional, a church deacon, a freemason, and many other selves inside. He starts to connect with each of these other selves, visualizing them, talking with them, establishing a connection with them. The addict must be reckoned with first, but reconnecting with other competent, and loved roles that shape his identity helped him regain a sense of balance. Also, some of his other subpersonalities can be marshaled to help him work with the addict. In his mind, Jorge's **father** *subpersonality has a conversation with the addict, reminding him of how much he wants to be a good parent to his kids. The* **church deacon** *can bolster his moral identity and help him forgive himself. Manuel was more than just the addict. The addict was only one part of him.*

Remembering that we are all a complex and rich system of selves helps to broaden and stabilize our identity. These subpersonalities are behaviorally very real, yet no single one ever defines us. Knowing this can often give us the courage to confront a part of ourselves that we would like to change.

Sometimes, we may **choose** to be out of balance with our full identity range because we are focusing on one subpersonality. In recovery, we may need to focus on the addict for a time. Yet, for a sustainable recovery, sooner or later, we need to reclaim the rest of who we are. It is appropriate for **the intern** to get the bulk of the time when completing medical school. But when we get older, this lack of balance has a price. I can't help but wonder how many "mid-life crises," are because suppressed aspects of ourselves come bursting out. The wider the range and the deeper the acceptance of **all of the selves within us**, the more profound we are as a person. We cannot evolve without acceptance of what is within us.[44]

IS THE RIGHT SUBPERSONALITY DOING THE JOB?

Here is another interesting relationship between outer roles (job functions) and subpersonalities. Given that we have a multiplicity of selves, is the right one doing the job? Can we choose which self we want to show up in a particular situation? Subpersonalities are also a storehouse of potential.

44 To deep dive further, we would recommend checking out our friend and colleague's book *Meet Your Inside Team: How to Turn Internal Conflict into Clarity and Move Forward with Your Life.* Speaking on an episode of the Relationship Matters podcast in 2022, Cynthia Loy Darst shared: "I think a lot of human beings don't realize that they have different aspects of their personality. You might hear of someone who says, 'This is just the way I am.' Okay. But have you ever just taken a moment to look at your thoughts about the way you are? To notice the parts of you that have you be this way. The more we know ourselves and have the ability to navigate our own inside team, the more effective we are in relationship with others."

It is useful to think of your ME system as a large house with many people living in it. The front door is the interface between the ME system and the outside world. Whoever is standing in the doorway has executive control over interacting with the real world. So, if I am talking with Marita, my spouse self is likely to be standing in the doorway, working with spouse roles. However, there are dozens of other selves within me. There is the psychologist, the bitch, the lover, the child of an alcoholic. Any of these selves may come to my doorway and emerge into interaction with the world, usually cued by the setting and situation. Most of these selves show up automatically. I don't have to consciously decide, "Now I am going to be my coach self." But some situations can trigger the wrong subpersonality to be in charge, depending on our history. At a Christmas party, a respected boss may turn into an unwelcome flirt. Alcohol has invited the wrong self to call the shots. It takes time and practice to be able to consciously choose which part of you will respond to a situation. Yet, with that time and practice, we can begin to shape which part of us will handle a situation.

Yukiko is a skilled nurse practitioner at a small hospital. Because of her competency, she is given the responsibility of managing the nursing night shift on her unit. This means she is responsible for supervising all the nursing decisions from 11 p.m. to 7 a.m. on her unit. Although she is a capable nurse, Yukiko is terrified on the nights she is in charge. She doubts herself, has trouble making decisions, and is stressed out the whole time. She does some subpersonality work and finds that her nurse practitioner self is having trouble showing up for the night shift. Instead, her inner ten-year-old kid is hijacking the situation. When Yukiko was ten, she was left in charge of her little sister when her mom had to go to work. Ten-year-old Yukiko felt overwhelmed by the responsibility of getting her little sister off to school. Now that Yukiko is an adult, the new job responsibilities are triggering

that ten-year-old to step into executive function during the night shift. The ten-year-old is a delightful little girl, but she is definitely the wrong person to be doing the job.

Once she realizes this, Yukiko works hard to create a relationship with her ten-year-old self. In her imagination, she reassures her internal child that it's not her job to supervise the hospital unit at night. It is not appropriate for a ten-year-old to be in charge. Yukiko spends time mentally reassuring that internal little girl and creating a relationship. She even creates an imaginary playroom where the child can hang out when Yukiko is at work. Before leaving for work, Yukiko tucks her up in the playroom and lets her know she's safe. Yukiko also works to encourage her experienced nurse practitioner subpersonality to show up at 11 p.m. when she starts her shift. That self has the knowledge and confidence to manage the floor. It takes time and patience, but Yukiko is able to teach her ten-year-old to stand down and have her nurse practitioner pick up the job. The ten-year-old is an automatic patterned response from Yukiko's past, but she has the EQ to work the dilemma through with her different subpersonalities.

SUBPERSONALITIES IN THE YOU/ME AND WE SYSTEM

When we interact with another person, they naturally bring their host of subpersonalities to the mix. This complexity becomes clear when two or more people must make a difficult, life-altering decision. Perhaps a couple is considering a divorce. The high stakes of such a decision are bound to generate strong subpersonalities in both partners. One self may be angry and just wants to walk out. Another self wonders if one more round of couples coaching will help. A third is agonized about the impact of the divorce on the kids. Both partners are cycling around these different selves and many others, so the sheer number of potential interactions between different selves is huge. And that's not even including all the external voices from the kids, the friends, the family! No wonder a big decision like this is messy and confusing.

WORKING WITH YOUR OWN SUBPERSONALITIES

Being able to effectively work with the members of your ME system is a fast track to personal evolution and harvesting all your potential. But how do we actually do that?

Reader, are you willing to cross an edge and learn about these different subpersonalities? Trust me; they are dying to meet you! We have trained hundreds of people to discover and work with their inner selves through the internal mansion exercise. By internal mansion, we just mean a large house; there should be no association with wealth or privilege. You just need a very big internal house to hold all the richness of your potential; it does not need to be fancy (unless it wants to be). We are going to check out your inside team by taking a tour of who lives in there. This exercise is a visualization that you will read through. You will want to take some notes, so have a pencil and paper handy.

RELATIONSHIP WARRIORSHIP EXERCISE: THE MANSION VISUALIZATION

Make yourself comfortable so that you can be relaxed and able to make some notes. Take your time as you read through the exercise, and imagine that each different subpersonality will come forward to meet you in their own way. Let go of figuring it out, and just allow what wants to emerge to come to you. There are no right answers or wrong answers in this exercise, just information.

In your mind's eye, let an image come to you of a very large house that lives inside of you. It is a house/mansion spacious enough for all your different selves to live in. Even from this distance, you know that this house is populated by many selves. Allow this house to form in your mind.

- What environment surrounds this house?
- What does it look like?
- How large or small is it?
- How luxurious or simple?
- When you are ready, write down a few words to describe it.

Now, approach your mansion/house and prepare to go in. You are here today to have a good look at the selves that live here. Let's head inside and look around in the public front room. How is it decorated? How big is it? When you are in public, what part or parts of you hang out in this entry hall? Take some notes about your discoveries.

There are many subpersonalities of different ages in your imaginary house. As you stand here in the entryway, BE your adult self, your body-age-today self. Know that each self you meet today is part of your creativeness, intelligence, and generativity! Now let's go on a tour of your mansion to meet some of the selves who share it together.

- First, find the room of your professional self. Who is that, and how are they dressed? What does their room look like? Introduce yourself to that person and be curious about them. What does your professional self **love** about what they do? Take some notes from your experience.

Now, find the room of a more outrageous self. Everyone has at least one! This is the one who secretly wants to sing opera, go to culinary school, or maybe be a stripper. It may be a part of you that a lot of people know about; it may be a part that you keep hidden. Often, this is a part that makes you smile. Find that person. Where does this subpersonality live? What do they have to say? Take notes.

So, the journey continues. It is time for you to visit with one of your most private, hidden selves. The one nobody knows about. Who is that? Take the time to find that person. You may not choose to share this self with anyone, and that's okay. Sometimes, there are parts of us that we are uncomfortable sharing. Go to that private self now. Why is this person hidden from the world? Who is this person that is locked away so carefully? What is the relationship like between you and that self? Take a few notes.

There are many, many rooms and selves that you could visit. Let's explore one more, maybe a self who wants to show up more in the world. This self is perhaps needed more in your life but hasn't been ready to come out yet. Who inside you is waiting to step more into your life? Why do you need that subpersonality, and what do they have to offer? Have a conversation with them. What support does that person need from you to be fully realized? Take some notes.

How many more rooms do you have in your house? Notice how much range you have! There are dozens of selves available to you, each with their own gifts. Even the ones that are hurt or traumatized are carrying part of your history. The more you know about all yourselves: the creative, the vulnerable, the triggered, the competent, the more you can work skillfully with yourself and with others. Check and see if there are any other parts of yourself that would like to meet you today. Have a conversation with them and take some notes.

- Finally, it is time to bring your attention back from that inward focus on your mansion, to the outward focus of the external world. Take a few moments to say goodbye to your internal house and everyone who lives there. Do it in the way that makes the most sense to you. When you are ready, gently bring your focus back to the room that you are in and this book you are reading. Make some final notes.

The mansion visualization is a great way to get to know some of the facets of your ME system. We believe that the number of selves available to us is limited only by our creativity. The whole of human experience lives within us, from the Buddha to the murderer, but these selves are split off from our experience. Evolution and healing occur when we begin to go into relationship with these different selves, when we can hear their stories and access their experience. The mansion visualization is useful as an introduction to your ME system and a gateway to exploring all the creative subpersonalities that live there. And, because we are human, we also have selves that are destructive or traumatized. Jorge had many positive selves, like the father and the deacon. He also had an addict. Yukiko had a strong nurse practitioner and a traumatized ten-year-old. All of our human experience lives within us, and all of it needs to be honored and cared for. Sometimes, when we do the mansion visualization, we find triggered parts of ourselves we don't feel competent to work with. This is useful information, and it can point us to the next step in our healing. Recognize if someone in your ME system needs help and get it for them. Talk to your coach or doctor and get a referral for trauma-based therapy based on your specific issue.

SUBPERSONALITIES AND GHOSTS AS ALLIES

Many years ago, I worked with a transgender man, Nico, who was invited to give a speech to a large psychological association on his experience of being transgender. He was terrified because he had never done any public speaking, and this was a deeply vulnerable topic. First, we located the selves inside him who had been deeply impacted by his journey. There were young female selves that had been shamed and silenced when they spoke about being a boy. There were confused adolescents, so overwhelmed by the pressure to conform that they were suicidal for many years. There was the proud man, which claimed his male identity and became a spokesperson for the transgender experience.

All these selves, both traumatized and empowered, had something important to contribute to his speech. The pain, hurt, and passion of these selves inspired him to want to speak for them. We also found and developed **a speaker** *self inside him, the one who would actually give the speech. He explored his memories of hearing people speaking powerfully about a personal transformation. These memories provided him with the outer and inner role qualities of how to be a great speaker. The speaker could use these qualities as a template for his own talk. Once the speaker felt empowered, he found he could speak for all of Nico's ME system.*

Working with his speaker helped to develop Nico, yet he still felt like it wasn't enough. He was taking a huge risk to speak publicly at this conference, and the exposure felt paralyzing. So, Nico developed an internal image for all the allies that would support him while he was giving his speech. He imagined standing at the podium, and behind him were hundreds of invisible transgender people who had suffered throughout history. Each transgender person supported the next by placing their hand on the shoulder of the person in front of them. The person at the head of the line placed their hands on Nico's shoulders. As he stood there giving his speech, he could feel the support of all the transgender people who had suffered terribly throughout history. He was speaking for them and for himself, and they poured their strength and wisdom into him. This image gave Nico the final sense of purpose and power that he needed. The speech was no longer about Nico; it was about speaking for hundreds of transgender people throughout the ages. They were empowering him to be their voice.

Doing subpersonality work is a rapid way for us to evolve all three types of system intelligences. Do you want to truly know your ME system? Use the Paper Constellation exercise shared in part one to give a voice and name to your subpersonalities on a particular topic. When you feel something strongly, ask yourself, **"Who is that?"** Let yourself develop an image, and most importantly, create a relationship with those selves. Have a conversation with them; they belong to you! Every aspect of your system has something to offer, even the parts you don't like.

Perhaps you want to be more skillful with someone? Remember, that person is also a gemstone with many facets as well. Some of these facets you may love, and other aspects you dislike. Can you forgive your partner for the part of them that is bossy, thick-skinned, or irritable? **That is only one part of them,** not the whole story of who they are.

Subpersonality work helps us to understand how many creative, crazy, colorful, and profound selves live within us. All of them are ME, yet none of them define me.

Assume that every part of you has a wisdom aspect, even the parts of you that you hate. I have an insecure and needy self, and the other, more independent parts of myself hated her. Yet, when I could bring myself to have a conversation with her, I could understand her. That young, insecure self carried painful memories of abandonment. She was letting me know that relationships were unpredictable and uncertain. In our conversations, I could validate her experience; relationships **are** uncertain and unpredictable while at the same time offering that there is no love without risk.

PART 3
EVOLUTION THROUGH RELATIONSHIP

EPILOGUE

"I-Thou is not a means to some object or goal, but a relation of presence involving the whole being of each subject."

– MARTIN BUBER

This book has explored many types of relationship systems in our lives. There is one more systemic relationship that we'd like to explore with you. Sadly, we believe it is an abusive relationship, one where there is very little Relationship Warriorship, Radical Responsibility, or Right Relationship. We are all abusers when it comes to our relationship with nature. I don't think I need to list the ways in which we poison, dominate, exterminate, and ignore the planet and all other kinds of living things upon it. We have all become numb to the litany of ecological disasters in our world. We read about it every day. We are experiencing it up close and personal as fires burn our homes or hurricanes flood our cities.

Make no mistake, our problem with the degradation of nature is a relationship issue. Nature is a complex system, and we believe that the skills and principles of this book can help us move towards Right Relationship with the planet. As discussed in the basics, the structure for this book is:

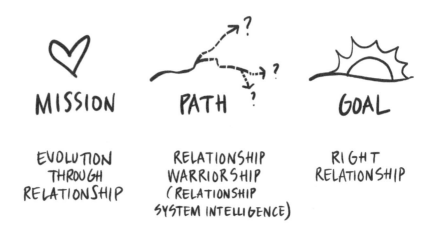

We must evolve in our relationship with nature if we and other species are going to survive. And, as with any relationship system, the path to Right Relationship runs through Relationship Warriorship and Relationship Systems Intelligence. Let's look at some of the attributes of Relationship Warriorship when we apply it to our relationship with nature.

Bravery. In Relationship Warriorship, the enemy is never another person or species; the enemy is always ignorance. Do we have the bravery to examine our own blindness about our impact on the globe? I am aware, in myself, of how hard it can be to stay open to looking at dying polar bears, plummeting bird populations, and the daily ecological disasters. It's just easier to turn away.

We need a George Floyd moment for nature. When George Floyd died, the litany of white-on-black murder reached a terrible tipping point. As white people, many of us could no longer bear to be paralyzed by our own ignorance. We didn't always know what to do, but we could not look away from the truth of systemic racial oppression. Acknowledging the pain of our separation from people of color and becoming informed about systemic racism is the beginning of the path. This opens the door to Radical Responsibility for changing the situation. Discerning and acting on what is uniquely mine to do is the path forward to racial Right Relationship.

Human beings also have their knee on the neck of nature. Relationship Warriorship begins with having the bravery to not look away. We can share our broken hearts and feelings of helplessness. We can reach out to nature and to each other and take Radical Responsibility, starting in own backyard.

Curiosity opens the path of educating myself. What aspect of nature do I **want** to learn about, not what I **should** learn about? Curiosity is the first step of connection. "What kind of bird is that? What is at the end of this forest trail? What is this bug in my yard?" All of these questions fuel delight.

Joy! Joy is the most important attribute of Relationship Warriorship. Our delight in nature can help us to stay open and engaged. Martin Buber, in his iconic book, *I and Thou*, speaks about how, when we love something, we **naturally become radically responsible for it.** We care for it because it is important to us. When we move into an I-Thou relationship with nature, it ceases to be an object to be manipulated. Instead, we move into Third Entity with it.

When we connect with the environment, we can open a profound treasure chest of gifts. There is so much evolutionary wealth available to us on every level of planetary life. **Nature heals the terrible loneliness we can feel in our hearts as a species.** Those of us who love our dogs, cats, and horses know the purity, delight, and intimacy those animals can bring us. A purring cat eases our soul. Running our hands through our dog's fur soothes us. But that sense of communion and exchange could be extended a thousand-fold by claiming personal relationship with **all** the plants and animals around us. Spy on the birds in your backyard. If you watch them, a window of wonder can open. Getting our hands in the garden dirt literally, physically raises our spirits.[45] We have been cut off from our most profound tribe, the plants and animals that are part of our extended family. If we are present and open to these beings, what gifts can they bring us? Relationship is reciprocal.

> *"I think it pisses God off if you walk by the color purple in a field somewhere and don't notice it. People think pleasing God is all God cares about. But any fool living in the world can see it always trying to please us back."*
>
> – ALICE WALKER, THE COLOR PURPLE

We are so impoverished regarding what plants and animals we are willing to love. Whole areas of animals, and especially insects, are discriminated against to the point of extinction. It is easy to soften our hearts when we see a koala or a baby seal. But what is our relationship with the ground squirrels when they eat our tomatoes? To the yellow jackets when they crash our picnic?

---

45 Christopher Lowry's 2007 study, "Identification of an Immune-Responsive Mesolimbocortical Serotonergic System: Potential Role in Regulation of Emotional Behavior," found that treatment with *M. vaccae*, a.k.a. soil bacterium, might have the same effect as anti-depressant drugs.

THE BLACK WIDOW IN THE GARAGE

*Last summer, I discovered a black widow living inside my garage door. Flooded with adrenaline, my brain was instantly triggered with a thousand narratives, all with exclamation points. "Those things are venomous! I have to kill it, or it will lay eggs! What if it bites one of the dogs!" But I stayed my hand long enough to calm down and get a tiny bit curious. I grudgingly noticed she was beautiful. About the size of a quarter ("That thing is huge!"), she had a shiny black bulbous body stamped with the iconic red hourglass. She sat on her web in a posture that made her hourglass always visible, warning the world. I left her alone, but for the next few months, she was a constant presence for me. Our relationship was difficult. Her presence showed me my own fear, murderousness, fascination, and respect. I looked for her every time I entered the garage, and every day was different. Each time, I stayed my hand until, many weeks later, I found her desiccated body. Some other spider had eaten her. I was hugely relieved, but also, vaguely bereft. That spider and I had a powerful connection. She woke me up and forced me to confront my human prejudice. **Any creature that threatens my comfort must die.***

Nobody is marching around out there with "insect rights" placards. If a creature scares us, if it is inconvenient, if it blocks something we want, we move to exterminate it. This is not Right Relationship. Does that mean I never kill bugs or trap rats in my house? Oh no, there are times I do choose to kill an animal. But now, harming any kind of creature is no longer automatic. If I kill the spider in my shower, I have to make the choice to do it rather than just automatically killing a **pest.** I am no longer ignorant. That black widow was a teacher, and I have come to understand that **all** nature is a teacher if we slow down and open to the exchange. Nature is always present, willing, and able to evolve the ME if we are willing to enter into a YOU/ME relationship with it.

Nature is a generous relationship partner. It wants to collaborate with its great storehouse of medicinal properties. The Yew tree in my front yard supplies a critical component of chemotherapy. The garden fox tail gives us digitalis. There is increasing evidence of the power of fungi in supporting the immune system.[46]

Nature is also generous with spiritual medicine our souls crave. Go forest bathing when you need a break. The filtered light, the smell of the rain, bird song, and local animals invite us into communion with them. We gain relief from our churning mind. We can also tap the WE system of plants and animals for insight.

JOANNE AND THE CHERRY TREE

Joanne got the news that her cancer had recurred and was now inoperable. During the fall, we coached together as she began to move from the path of illness to the path of dying. Outside her bedroom window was a large cherry tree that was turning a brilliant yellow. There were also several luminous red maples. When invited into communion with those trees, Joanne realized they had something to teach her. The brilliance of that cherry tree was broad-casting a message. "Before letting go, celebrate! Flaunt the unique colors that have made you who you are. You are gold, and red, and russet. Shine out your secret colors that have been beneath the surface. Celebrate!"

---

46 In the 2008 TED talk "6 ways mushrooms can save the world," that's had over eight million views, Fungi expert Paul Stamet shared that, "preserving the genome of these fungi in the old-growth forest I think is absolutely critical for human health. I've been involved with the U.S. Defense Department BioShield program. We submitted over 300 samples of mushrooms that were boiled in hot water, and mycelium, harvesting these extracellular metabolites. And a few years ago, we received these results. We have three different strains of Agarikon mushrooms that were highly active against poxviruses. Dr. Earl Kern, who's a smallpox expert of the U.S. Defense Department, states that any compounds that have a selectivity index of two or more are active. 10 or greater are considered to be very active. Our mushroom strains were in the highly active range."

Still, later, that tree taught her how to let go. "Notice the leaves spiraling down, one or two at a time. Releasing can be a slow and effortless process. Let go gently, little by little."

Nature is constantly available in our backyard, in our local park, or in the form of pets and plants. We don't have to drive to a wilderness area to find its wonder. Create a connection with your local living things. Get curious. And don't do this **just to save the planet.** Do it because being in relationship with nature will save **you!** It will slow you down, create an intimate connection, heal your heart, and open a portal to the divine. As we struggle to take responsibility for the planet, we already know that guilt won't get us there. Passion for something we love will get us there. We naturally care for the things that are precious to us. Develop a passionate dialogue with your backyard, your local park, your region.

Relationship is about communication. Speak with your environment and let it answer you. Make these places your ally and let them tell you how to take better care of them. Your local stream may ask you to pick up the trash around it. Local birds may suggest you plant Black-Eyed Susan in your garden because birds like the seeds. Before you squash that bug in your kitchen, what does it have to say to you? Right Relationship begins with listening to your partner. Pay attention. Nature needs you to listen! Let it inform you of what is yours to do.

The Relationship Warriorship attribute of **commitment** is the glue of any kind of relationship. This doesn't have to be a "till death do us part" kind of commitment. It can be a weekly commitment to replenish the bird feeder. Start with something small, doable, and pleasurable. When I take a walk, I take a small trash bag and pick up any litter I find on the way. It's a tiny action, but it is a daily commitment. It is a small way I express my love for my neighborhood.

Can we **reduce our armor** in the face of climate change? When things feel hopeless, it is so easy to withdraw or get defensive. Or we could open to the piercing beauty of the world and let it touch us. How do we stay involved with climate change in a way that doesn't make us turn away because we feel helpless? The exercise below provides us with a way of accessing the wisdom of nature. Nature longs to be in a relationship with us; let it be your coach!

RELATIONSHIP WARRIORSHIP EXERCISE: NATURE AS ALLY[47]

This is a simple guided imagery exercise that helps us open up to nature as an ally.

- Think of a disturbance or difficulty in your life.

- Now, set that disturbance aside.

- Remember a place in nature that is important to you, someplace that gives you delight and ease. Take your time to think of the right place.

- In your imagination, let yourself be there fully in your nature place. Pay attention to what is there. What can you see around you? What do you hear? Where are you standing, and what is the weather? Breathe deeply. What do you notice about the air?

- Relax deeply into this place. It is **your** place; enjoy it for a few moments.

---

47 This is taken from the Nature Connection retreat that was created by Faith Fuller and Janet Frood for CRR Global USA during the COVID-19 pandemic. This one-day virtual retreat explored how nature can be a support and ally in a volatile, world and engage in practices that help us reconnect with the wisdom of nature.

- Open up to the possibility that this nature place has its own wisdom, and it would like to be your ally.

- Now, recall the disturbance that we asked to think of at the beginning of the exercise and bring it with you to this nature place.

- Fully experience your nature spot while sharing your disturbance with it. What do you notice? What is in the nature spot that might have something to offer you about your disturbance? Let some sight, sound, or experience of the scenery speak to you. Take your time. There might be more than one message.

- Soon, you will be returning to the regular world. Is there an action or insight you want to take back with you as a result of your experience?

- Now, gently return to this book. Take a minute to write down any insights about your experience.

Nature is the ultimate system. Our relationship with it is a natural extension of this book. Whatever we care about, we also need to care for.

CONCLUSION

"Whether we are looking to create closeness with others, with nature, or with the living mystery, an invitational presence is the prerequisite to any form of intimacy."

– TOKO-PA TURNER

The motivation for this book is grief and passion. Grief because we all feel the pain of global wars, climate change, racism, and our inability to just get along. We are also separated from our tribe of fellow living creatures. It feels like we are starving, emotionally and physically, amid plenty.

This book is also passionate because it is driven by the longing and the belief that **we can** evolve into a more skillful connection. We live our lives in ever-widening gyres of relationship. We are the only species capable of relating to **all** living things, from viruses to nations. We are the only species with a capacity to listen to, appreciate, and connect with **all** types of people if we choose. We need the will to commit to Relationship Warriorship, and we need the Relationship Systems Intelligence tools and skills to exercise that will.

Finally, we need the dream and joy of Right Relationship to pull us forward. And so, I return to you, reader. What are **your** dreams for relationship in your life? What is the passion, grief, and joy that can pull you forward to become a Relationship Warrior? Do you long to be a better leader, a loving father? What is the particular relationship you would like to evolve? What part of this book would be most helpful to you for that? May your heart pull you forward, and your curiosity educate you on your evolutionary path in relationship.

ABOUT
CRR GLOBAL

Our Vision: Relationship matters, from humanity to nature, to the larger whole.

Our Mission: The world is our work. We create positive change together, facing up to humanity's greatest challenges, one relationship system at a time.

We believe leadership is a role belonging to the system, showing up in the most unlikely places from the most unlikely people. We know that together we can make the world a more inclusive and diverse place, from the living room to the boardroom—for families, communities, and organizations. At CRR Global, we are on a passionate mission to make our students' and clients' relationship systems aware by providing world-class training and thought leadership.

We leverage the collective power and wisdom of our faculty and partners to empower the families, communities, and organizations we touch. We have trained over 20,000 practitioners, who in turn spread the word across six continents in numerous countries

For more information, visit **www.crrglobal.com**

CRR GLOBAL TRAINING

This book draws heavily on the teaching and practices of Organization and Relationship Coaching (ORSC). ORSC is the flagship program of CRR Global, specializing in working with relationship systems such as teams, organizations, families and communities. ORSC is a powerful coach training program that puts systemic interdependence and relationships in the foreground. Over the last two decades, CRR Global has trained over 20,000 practitioners worldwide, ranging from the Americas to Asia, from Europe to Africa, the Middle East and Australia. And the demand is growing.

ABOUT THE AUTHOR

FAITH FULLER PHD, ORSCC, CPC

Faith is the former President of CRR Global. She is a psychologist and experienced trainer and coach, with over thirty years of experience working with organizations, couples, and communities.

Faith takes a systems approach to coaching, namely that all aspects of the system need to be addressed for effective change to occur.

Her particular skill is empowering powerful, productive, and joyous relationships in couples, partnerships, and teams. She has a background in consultation, team building, conflict resolution, and community crisis intervention.

Some of her clients include: YMCA, Oakland Interagency Children's Policy Council, Horizon Services Inc., Bristol Hospital (England), Monkton Wilde Center (England), Beacon Schools, Boeing, The Coaches Training Institute, Narcotics Education League, Mandana House, Vocolot Performances, Highland Health Psych. Center, and Perry Point VA Center.

ACKNOWLEDGMENTS

Faith and Marita are proud to carry the title of Founders of CRR Global and the Organization and Relationship Systems Coaching Program (ORSC). At the same time, Founder is just an external role that encompasses the contributions of hundreds of people to this work. ORSC does not belong to us; we have simply had the privilege to integrate many different strands of relationship wisdom.

We would like to offer deep appreciation and respect to the individuals and organizations that contributed to this work. Special thanks to Arnold and Any Mindell and the Process Work Center that opened our eyes to the beauty and power of unfolding signals. The Co-Active Training Institute gave us the coaching stance and structures we needed to create a Coaching organization.

There are several individuals who helped to midwife this book. Pamela van den Berg, a skilled graphic illustrator, graciously created the wonderful illustrations for this book. Howard VanEs and his team at Let's Write Books helped me to navigate the complexities of producing a book. I offer a special shout-out to Katie Churchman, whose enthusiasm, clear thinking, and editing skills brought this book alive. Truly this book would not exist without her! Finally, a bow of appreciation to Meredith Fuller Luyten, who spent two weeks honing the content and style of this book. Her writing experience and wisdom were invaluable.

Most of all, we want to honor the thousands of students and faculty who have left their mark on this work. Their insights, criticisms, and additions have clarified the concepts and honed the tools. Our students showed us that there is no area of life that does not require relationship skills. We have trained clergy, corporates, medical personal, educators, government personnel, real estate agents, and many other types of professionals. They opened our eyes to the specific application of relationship systems to **their** industry. We know they will carry the work forward and continue to evolve it.

BIBLIOGRAPHY

Anita Raghavan, K., & Barrionuevo, A. (2002, August 26). "How Enron Bosses Created A Culture of Pushing Limits." The Wall Street Journal. https://www.wsj.com/articles/SB1030320285540885115

Bell, L. (2016, August 28). "What is Moore's Law? WIRED explains the theory that defined the tech industry." WIRED UK. https://www.wired.co.uk/article/wired-explains-moores-law

Boroditsky, L. (2018, May 2). "How language shapes the way we think." https://www.youtube.com/watch?v=RKK7wGAYP6k

Brach, T. (2015, June 1). "The Lion's Roar." Psychology Today. https://www.psychologytoday.com/us/blog/finding-true-refuge/201506/the-lion-s-roar

Brown, Brené. (2020). *Gifts of Imperfection*. Random House Publishing Group.

Brown, Brené. (2015). *Daring Greatly: How the Courage to be Vulnerable Transforms The Way We Live, Love, Parent, and Lead*. Penguin Books Ltd.

Buber, M. (2020). *I and Thou*. Clydesdale Press.

Churchman, K. (n.d.). "Relationship Matters." Relationship Matters Podcast. https://relationshipmatters.buzzsprout.com/

Clifton, J. (2022, August 11). "The World's workplace is broken—here's how to fix it." Gallup.com. https://www.gallup.com/workplace/393395/world-workplace-broken-fix.aspx

Cook-Greuter, S. R. (1985). "Ego development: Nine levels of increasing embrace - integral art lab." Ego Development: Nine Levels of Increasing Embrace. https://integralartlab.com/wp-content/uploads/2020/12/9-levels-of-increasing-embrace-update-1-07.pdf

Cook-Greuter, S. R. (2004). "Making the case for a developmental perspective." *Industrial and Commercial Training, 36*(7), 275–281. https://doi.org/10.1108/00197850410563902

Cook-Greuter, S. R., & Soulen, J. (2007). "The developmental perspective in Integral Counseling." Counseling and Values, *51*(3), 180–192. https://doi.org/10.1002/j.2161-007x.2007.tb00077.x

CPP Global. (2008, July). "Workplace Conflict and how businesses can harness it to thrive." CPP Global Human Capital Report. http://img.en25.com/Web/CPP/Conflict_report.pdf

Cross, R. (2019, September 10). "To Be Happier at Work, Invest More in Your Relationships." Harvard Business Review. https://hbr.org/2019/07/to-be-happier-at-work-invest-more-in-your-relationships

Csikszentmihalyi, M. (2009). *Flow: The Psychology of Optimal Experience.* Harper and Row.

Darst, C. L. (2018). *Meet Your Inside Team: How to Turn Internal Conflict into Clarity and Move Forward with Your Life.*

Davies, J. B., & Shorrocks, A. F. (2018, December). "Comparing global inequality of income and wealth." United Nations University. https://www.wider.unu.edu/sites/default/files/Publications/Working-paper/PDF/wp2018-160.pdf

"Devastatingly pervasive: 1 in 3 women GLOBALLY experience violence." WHO. (2021). https://www.who.int/news/item/09-03-2021-devastatingly-pervasive-1-in-3-women-globally-experience-violence

The DISC Profile. Discprofile.com. (n.d.). https://www.discprofile.com/what-is-disc/disc-styles

Duhigg, C. (2016, February 25). "What Google Learned From Its Quest to Build the Perfect Team." The New York Times. https://www.nytimes.com/2016/02/28/magazine/what-google-learned-from-its-quest-to-build-the-perfect-team.html

Felsenthal, E. (2020, April 9). "Front Line Workers Tell Their Own Stories in the New Issue of TIME." Time. https://time.com/5434949/divorce-rate-children-marriage-benefits/)

Freke, T. (2002). *Tao: Book and Card Pack.* Godsfield.

Fridjhon, M., & Fuller, F. (2016). "Creating Coaching Cultures." CRR Global. https://crrglobal.com/wp-content/uploads/attachments/creating_coaching_cultures_guide.2016_4.pdf

Fuller, F., & Fridjhon, M. (2016). *Creating Coaching Cultures.* CRR Global. https://crrglobal.com/wp-content/uploads/attachments/creating_coaching_cultures_guide.2016_4.pdf.

Fuller, F., & Fridjhon, M. (2022, June 3). CRR Global. https://crrglobal.com/

Fuller, F., & Frood, J. (2021). "Nature connection retreat: Virtual and experiential." CRR Global USA | Home of ORSCTM | Coach Training Programs. https://www.crrglobalusa.com/nature.html

Gelfand, M. J. (2020). *Rule Makers, Rule Breakers: Tight and Loose Cultures and the Secret Signals That Direct Our Lives.* Robinson.

Goleman, D. (2004, January). "What Makes a Leader?" Harvard Business Review. https://hbr.org/2004/01/what-makes-a-leader

Goleman, D. (2015). *Focus: The Hidden Driver of Excellence.* Harper.

Goleman, D. (2020). *Emotional Intelligence.* Bantam Books.

Goleman, D., Boyatzis, R. E., & McKee, A. (2013). "Primal leadership: unleashing the power of emotional intelligence." Harvard Business Review Press.

Gottman, J. M., & Silver, N. (2018). *The Seven Principles for Making Marriage Work.* Cassell Illustrated.

Guardian News and Media. (2021, May 24). "Most Republicans still Believe 2020 election was stolen from Trump – Poll." The Guardian. https://www.theguardian.com/us-news/2021/may/24/republicans-2020-election-poll-trump-biden

Guttman, H. M. (2008). *Great Business Teams: Cracking the Code for Standout Performance.* John Wiley & Sons.

Hajela, D. (2011, September 9). "Cantor Fitzgerald: Surviving 9/11 and Thriving." NBC New York. https://www.nbcnewyork.com/news/local/september-11-anniversary-cantor-fitzgerald-911/1928219/

Harvard Second Generation Study. Harvard. (n.d.). https://www.adultdevelopmentstudy.org/

Hedges, C. (2003, July 6). "What Every Person Should Know About War." The New York Times. https://www.nytimes.com/2003/07/06/books/chapters/what-every-person-should-know-about-war.html

Hosch, W. L. (n.d.). "Moore's law." Encyclopaedia Britannica. https://www.britannica.com/technology/Moores-law

Ingham, H., & Luft, J. (1955). "The Johari window, a graphic model of inter-personal awareness, Proceedings of the Western training laboratory in group development (dissertation)." UCLA, Los Angeles, CA.

Institute, C.-A. T. (2022, October 21). "Co-Active - leadership training & life coaching certification." Co-Active Training. https://coactive.com/

International Coaching Federation (ICF). (2019, October). "Updated ICF Core Competency Model - Coach Federation." Updated ICF Core Competency Model. https://coachfederation.org/app/uploads/2019/11/ICFCompetencyModel_Oct2019.pdf

Jorgensen, H.-H., Bruehl, O., & Franke, N. (2014, August). "Making change work . . . while the work keeps changing How Change Architects lead and manage organizational change." IBM. https://www.ibm.com/downloads/cas/WA3NR3NM

Katie, B. (n.d.). *The Official Website for The Work of Byron Katie.* The Work of Byron Katie. https://thework.com/

Katie, B., & Mitchell, S. (2003). *Loving What Is: Four Questions That Can Change Your Life.* Three Rivers Press.

Kegan, R. (1998). *In Over Our Heads.* https://doi.org/10.2307/j.ctv1pncpfb

Kegan, R. (2009). *The Evolving Self.* https://doi.org/10.2307/j.ctvjz81q8

Kegan, R., & Lahey, L. L. (2009). "Immunity to change: How to overcome it and unlock potential in yourself and your organization." Harvard Business School.

Kegan, R., Lahey, L. L., Miller, M. L., Fleming, A., & Helsing, D. (2016). "An everyone culture: Becoming a deliberately developmental organization." Harvard Business Review Press.

Kornfield, J. (2002). *A Path with Heart.* Bantam Books.

Kübler-Ross, E. (1978). *On Death and Dying.* Macmillan Publ. Co.

Lama, D. (2021, September 6). *Compassion as the Source of Happiness.* The 14th Dalai Lama. https://www.dalailama.com/messages/compassion-and-human-values/compassion-as-the-source-of-happiness

"The Leadership Circle Profile 360 Leadership Assessment." Leadership Circle. (2022, August 3). https://leadershipcircle.com/en/leadership-assessment-tools/leadership-circle-profile/

Leadership IQ. (n.d.). "Internal Locus of Control: Definition and Research." Leadership IQ. https://www.leadershipiq.com/blogs/leadershipiq/internal-locus-of-control-definition-and-research

Lowry, C. A., Hollis, J. H., de Vries, A., Pan, B., Brunet, L. R., Hunt, J. R. F., Paton, J. F. R., van Kampen, E., Knight, D. M., Evans, A. K., Rook, G. A. W., & Lightman, S. L. (2007). "Identification of an immune-responsive mesolimbocortical serotonergic system: Potential role in regulation of emotional behavior." Neuroscience, 146(2), 756–772. https://doi.org/10.1016/j.neuroscience.2007.01.067

Magnolia Pictures. (2005). *Enron: The Smartest Guys in the Room.*

Making Change Work. IBM Global Business Services. (2008, May). https://www.ibm.com/downloads/cas/2EXR3WMA

Miller, E. (2013, December 27). "9 Ways To Cultivate Wisdom And Compassion." HuffPost. https://www.huffpost.com/entry/spiritual-development_b_4152726

Mindell, Amy. (2003). *Metaskills: The Spiritual Art of Therapy.* Lao Tse Press.

Mindell, Arnold, & Mindell, A. (2016). *Riding the Horse Backwards: Process Work in Theory and Practice.* Lao Tse Press.

Mindell, Arnold. (1993). *The Shaman's Body.* Harper.

Mindell, Arnold. (2000). *Dreaming While Awake: Techniques for 24-Hour Lucid Dreaming.* Hampton Roads.

Mindell, Arnold. (2001). *The Dreammaker's Apprentice: Using Heightened States of Consciousness to Interpret Dreams.* Hampton Roads Pub. Co.

Mindell, Arnold. (2002). *The Deep Democracy of Open Forums: Practical Steps to Conflict Prevention and Resolution for the Family, Workplace, and World.* Hampton Roads Publishing.

Mindell, Arnold. (2012). *Quantum Mind: The Edge Between Physics and Psychology.* Deep Democracy Exchange.

Mindell, Arnold. (2014). *Sitting in the Fire: Large Group Transformation Using Conflict and Diversity*. Deep Democracy Exchange.

Mineo, L. (2018, November 26). "Over nearly 80 years, Harvard study has been showing how to live a healthy and happy life." Harvard Gazette. https://news.harvard.edu/gazette/story/2017/04/over-nearly-80-years-harvard-study-has-been-showing-how-to-live-a-healthy-and-happy-life/

The Myer Briggs Company. (n.d.). *The Myers-Briggs Company*. Official Myers Briggs Personality Test. https://www.themyersbriggs.com/en-US/Products-and-Services/Myers-Briggs

Nelson, P. (2018). *There's a Hole in My Sidewalk: The Romance of Self-Discovery*. Atria Paperbacks.

Nichols, M. P., & Davis, S. D. (2019). *Family Therapy: Concepts and Methods*. Pearson.

Nussbaum, D. (2019, January 17). "Tight and Loose CULTURES: A conversation with Michele Gelfand." Behavioral Scientist. https://behavioralscientist.org/tight-and-loose-cultures-a-conversation-with-michele-gelfand/

Pappas, S. (2022, October 17). "Are flat-earthers being serious?" LiveScience. https://www.livescience.com/24310-flat-earth-belief.html

Person. (2021, May 24). "53% of Republicans view Trump as true U.S. president – Reuters/Ipsos." Reuters. https://www.reuters.com/world/us/53-republicans-view-trump-true-us-president-reutersipsos-2021-05-24/

Rød, A., & Fridjhon, M. (2020). *Creating Intelligent Teams: Leading with Relationship Systems Intelligence*. KR Publishing.

Seppälä, E., & Cameron, K. (2017, May 8). "Proof that positive work cultures are more productive." Harvard Business Review. https://hbr.org/2015/12/proof-that-positive-work-cultures-are-more-productive

Shenk, J. W. (2009, June). "What Makes Us Happy?" The Atlantic. https://www.theatlantic.com/magazine/archive/2009/06/what-makes-us-happy/307439/

Smolin, L. (n.d.). "Time is FUNDAMENTAL, space is EMERGENT – why physicists are rethinking REALITY: Aeon Videos." Aeon. https://aeon.co/videos/time-is-fundamental-space-is-emergent-why-physicists-are-rethinking-reality

Stamet, P. (n.d.). *Funghi Perfecti*. Fungi Perfecti. https://fungi.com/

Stamets, P. (2008). "6 ways mushrooms can save the world | TED Talk." Paul Stamets. https://www.ted.com/talks/paul_stamets_6_ways_mushrooms_can_save_the_world/transcript?language=en

TalentSmartEQ. (2021). *Emotional Intelligence Training, Coaching, & Assessment.* TalentSmart inc. https://www.talentsmarteq.com/

Tennov, D. (1999). *Love and Limerence: The Experience of Being in Love.* Scarecrow Press.

"Trump badly losing his fights with media - public policy polling." Public Policy Polling. (2017, February). https://www.publicpolicypolling.com/wp-content/uploads/2017/09/PPP_Release_National_22417.pdf

Trungpa, C., & Gimian, C. R. (2004). *Shambhala: The Sacred Path of the Warrior.* Shambhala.

U.S. Bureau of Labor Statistics. (n.d.). *"Survival of private sector establishments by opening year."* U.S. Bureau of Labor Statistics. https://www.bls.gov/bdm/us_age_naics_00_table7.txt

Vaillant, G. E. (2015). *Triumphs of Experience: The Men of the Harvard Grant Study.* The Belknap Press of Harvard University Press.

Vazquez, M., & Kelly, C. (2020, February 28). "Trump says coronavirus will 'disappear' eventually." CNN. https://www.cnn.com/2020/02/27/politics/trump-coronavirus-disappear/index.html

Walker, A. (2022). *The Color Purple.* Weidenfeld & Nicolson.

Walt Disney Studios Home Entertainment. (2015). *Inside Out.* Milano.

Weerd, F. U. de, & Fridjhon, M. (2021). *Systems Inspired Leadership: How to Tap Collective Wisdom to Navigate Change, Enhance Agility, And Foster Collaboration.* CRR Global.

"What is company culture? [updated for 2021] - indeed." Indeed. (n.d.). https://www.indeed.com/hire/c/info/business-in-culture

Wheatley, M. J. (2006). *Leadership and the New Science.* Berrett-Koehler Publishers.

Wilding, M. (2020, January 21). "Successful People Have A Strong 'Locus of Control.' Do You?" Forbes. https://www.forbes.com/sites/melodywilding/2020/03/02/successful-people-have-a-strong-locus-of-control-do-you/?sh=500723187af3

Workplace Conflict Statistics & The Cost of Conflict at Work: PPS. Pollack Peacebuilding Systems. (2021, July 2). https://pollackpeacebuilding.com/workplace-conflict-statistics/